Retrain Your *Brain* for *Joy*

31 Mini-Adventures

MARY HENDERSON

WESTBOW PRESS
A DIVISION OF THOMAS NELSON & ZONDERVAN

WestBow Press books may be ordered through booksellers or by contacting:
WestBow Press
A Division of Thomas Nelson & Zondervan
1663 Liberty Drive
Bloomington, IN 47403
www.westbowpress.com
1 (866) 928-1240

ISBN: 978-1-4908-5617-9 (sc)
ISBN: 978-1-4908-5616-2 (hc)
ISBN: 978-1-4908-5618-6 (e)

Library of Congress Control Number: 2014918404

Printed in the United States of America.

WestBow Press rev. date: 11/11/2014

For the One who gave me life and who is my daily delight.

Contents

INTRODUCTION

Come on an Adventure!

> Rise up, my love, my fair one, and come away. For lo, the winter is past, the rain is over and gone. The flowers appear on the earth; the time of singing has come, And the voice of the turtledove is heard in our land. The fig tree puts forth her green figs, and the vines with the tender grapes give a good smell. Rise up, my love, my fair one, and come away! (Song 2:10–13NKJV)

Imagine going through each day of your life significantly happier than you are right now. Wherever you are in life's circumstances, whether facing minor or major obstacles, whether battling through difficulties related to school, job, family, illness, or relationships, most of us would like to find a way to experience greater joy and fulfillment, despite our circumstances.

I'd like to invite you upon a thirty-one-day adventure to learn to experience life with increasing levels of happiness and well-being amidst your circumstances. This adventure doesn't involve taking a magical modern pill. This experience has been around for centuries—even millennia. It's what the apostle Paul wrote about around AD 61 from a prison cell, suffering beatings, impoverishment, and criticism. "Whatever is true, whatever is honorable, whatever is right, whatever is pure, whatever is lovely, whatever is of good repute, if there is any excellence and if anything worthy of praise, dwell on these things" (Phil. 4:8 NASB). In a similar vein, he wrote to the Thessalonians, "Be joyful always, pray continually, give thanks in all circumstances" (1 Thess. 5:16–18 NIV).

But how do we firmly embed this habitual mindset into our day-to-day experience? Researchers tell us it takes a month of daily practice to acquire a consistent habit. The thirty-one activities in the following pages are designed to accomplish exactly that. Each mini-adventure involves a simple, experience-oriented learning activity that can be easily incorporated throughout your day. Collectively, they're designed to help you learn to proactively notice and savor the positive in your life, rather than magnetically being drawn to focus upon the negative.

Before embarking upon any adventure, however, it's important to be aware of a few potential pitfalls. Retraining your brain to dwell upon the positive is important for anyone seeking greater joy, but it's only one significant ingredient in the recipe for overall mental well-being. The foundational ingredient is a personal relationship with God that's continually growing and deepening through your relationship with Him and others. This relationship involves relying on His Spirit to transform you and create lasting change. (You can read more about this in the last two chapters of this book.) Many people today are facing major issues related to life difficulties or personal growth needs. That's why it's important to incorporate into your life important ingredients like counseling, supportive friends, and other specific, need-related input.

Here are some important tools that can be vitally helpful for the success of your thirty-one-day adventure:

1. Companionship. Invite a friend, spouse, family members, or group to venture with you over the next thirty-one days. You could talk about your adventures at the end of the day around a meal or enlist some Facebook or Twitter companions. If you're in counseling, include this as part of your weekly session. Involving others enables you to be consistent each day, and it will enhance and elucidate your experience. Plus, it will just be more fun!
2. Journaling. It's also crucial that you write about your experiences each day, even if only briefly. In this book, a blank page is provided after each activity, or you might prefer to buy a small notebook for daily entries. Along with the book, there's a card for each day to carry with you as a reminder. You can also jot notes on the back of it. Writing helps you to notice and remember all of your observations, to more fully embed them into your mind, to look back over the day with greater joy and

enrichment, and to more effectively establish your new habitual mindset.

3. Reminders. Each daily mini-adventure involves briefly noticing or contemplating things throughout your day. Most people need something to jog their minds to do this. You might post stick-up notes in crucial locations or wear a special bracelet or ring as a continual reminder. One person put a small ink mark on her hand that would grab her attention during the day. Or simply bringing your book, journal, or note card wherever you go may serve this purpose. Any of these suggestions will help you toward your goal of remembering to choose joy as a way of life.
4. Forethought. There are a few mini-adventures that might take brief forethought or planning. Look ahead at days 10, 18, 19, 24, and 28 to see if you'd like to do a little preparation, although none is required. For example, Days 10 and 18 involve looking for opportunities to give to others in small, practical ways. This means being with people on those days. So if Days 10 and 18 fall at times when you'll mostly be home alone, exchange those days for others. But make sure to remember them the next time your days involve people. Write them on your calendar in advance so you don't miss out on joyful experiences. Day 19 involves choosing music, and Day 28 might involve a camera if you'd like, which could mean a little preparation. Finally, your adventures on Day 24 may require a slightly flexible schedule. But remember, this book is designed to easily incorporate into your daily life. Too much preparation could defeat the joy of its simplicity.
5. Prayer. Pray at the start of the day for each activity. Pray for the Holy Spirit to be transforming you through each mental adventure. Pray for God to guide your thoughts throughout the day regarding that activity. Pray that a joyful mind will become your lifelong daily habit. Pray for your overall success in this adventure, and thank God as you see it happening.

One final concern. There may be some adventurers embarking upon this journey who'll worry about focusing on themselves too much in this area of inner joy. But the simple fact is that in all areas, Jesus' followers are to think and act in accordance with what's true. We need to regard ourselves in accordance with the truth. Some may say, *Don't think about yourself at all.* And yet, without inward reflection and awareness, we may be operating with subconscious perspectives that are untrue and that continually trip us up. For example, a devoted, hard-working Christian may be acting out of underlying, subconscious beliefs that tell him he needs to earn his worth or standing before God. This idea stands in stark contrast to the Christian who knows he's deeply loved, God's valuable masterpiece, and completely right before God. Therefore, these things flow out of his life into joyful service to God and others. It's this latter mindset that the self-related exercises are designed to create.

Now having said all these things, have fun! The adventure you're embarking upon can be like playing a game throughout your day. You'll be creating a secret inner life that keeps you smiling inwardly through even mundane tasks. And all along, you'll be transforming your mindset, renewing your mind, and creating a joyful, lifelong habit. So onward and upward into the light!

THE ADVENTURES

Week 1

A Lifestyle of Joy: Principle 1—Noticing and Savoring

"Two men looked out through prison bars,
One saw mud, the other stars."

—Oscar Wilde

Today, there's a lot I could be depressed about.

1. It's pouring rain outside. I absolutely love the sun. I need to go to the store today because we have very little to eat; the cupboards are bare. I hate it when I let that happen. But in the pouring rain, I don't think I'll be going to the store today.
2. I have three grown children, and one of them is going through something that has me really concerned. Something every mother would be worried about. Something your mind can go back to repeatedly and dwell on.
3. My husband is across the Atlantic Ocean in Budapest, Hungary on one of his regular work trips for two weeks. I'm lonely.
4. My fibromyalgia is acting up in my hands and arms. I never know exactly what brings on a flare-up, and it's a tricky process getting it to calm down.
5. One of my sons recently rejoined the military. He loves dangerous assignments. This is something I prayed about and fought against because of concern for his welfare. If I let myself think about it, I can be terribly worried and fearful. After all, I already struggled and prayed through his previous four years in the Marines.

Yet, despite all these things, I feel buoyantly joyful and at peace. In my own way, I'm looking out through prison bars, and instead of seeing mud, I see stars.

1. Because, even though I love the sun and don't like rain, my trees and plants are so happy to receive this moisture into their parched beings. And so are everyone's lawns and plants around me. We've been going through drought conditions in my area for the past two years. This rain is life-giving.
2. About that grown child who is going through difficult times: I've talked to God so much about this situation and have felt God's sweet truths and reassurances in this process. Not only has it drawn me closer to God, but closer to my husband, as we talk and pray together. There's no other person in the world with whom I share this deep, binding concern for our three treasured children. It weaves our hearts closer together.
3. Regarding that husband, absence makes the heart grow fonder. Like other couples, we've discovered that time and space apart makes us appreciate each other more. Also, these trips provide us with time to work intently on our different projects. Then, we're delighted to see each other again when he gets back from his trips to Eastern Europe.
4. Concerning my fibromyalgia, although I still have aches and pains, I'm immensely grateful to have come so far. I'm no longer in a wheelchair, no longer disabled. As a result, I'm filled with joy and gratitude.
5. Regarding my military son, he's doing what he has so passionately wanted to do for years. Just the process of being assigned to his current military position was a huge challenge, endeavor, and honor. How can I not be happy with him? He's thriving spiritually, experiencing God on a deep level. How can I not be glad?

We all look out through our own types of prison bars in life, and sometimes, in some seasons, those prison bars are thicker and heavier than at other times. What have we trained ourselves to focus upon? Mud or stars? Our answer to that question can largely determine whether we are gloomy and anxious or peaceful and positive.

So stop right now, and grab a pen and paper. First, write a list of ten things you're thankful for. After you've done that, write down ten more things. Finally, write down ten more.

Now take a moment to reflect upon your lists. Is it surprising that you have so many positive things in your life? Why not begin to focus upon positive things, and even choose a new lens in order to drastically improve your daily peace and contentment?

Our goal is to retrain our brains into a new habit of automatically focusing upon the positive, resulting in a lot more joy and gratitude. This will involve a systematic process because we're in the habit of just letting our minds decide how big or small to make things and where to put our focus. We need to take the reins of our minds, and through practice, grow in the habit of redirecting our focus and perception.

I think this is part of what Paul was talking about in Romans 12:2 when he wrote, "And do not be conformed to this world, but be transformed by the renewing of your mind." One aspect of renewing our minds is training them to perceive differently and to focus differently. In a similar vein, I think Paul was referring to this in Philippians 4:8 when he encouraged people to retrain and renew their minds to dwell upon what is true, noble, right, etc. Without retraining and renewing, our unruly minds wander to whatever perspectives they inadvertently settle upon, which are often negative.

This brings us to something I like to call *noticing and savoring.* (You'll have many opportunities in this book to practice these skills.) This phrase simply means that, as you go through your day, the mini-adventures will help you to develop the habit of noticing what's good and savoring that for a few seconds or minutes.

How do we define the verb notice? Noticing can be defined in the following way: to become aware of, observe, perceive, note, or detect.

Our mini-adventures are going to hone your skill of noticing. You'll start to become aware of things in your surroundings that you didn't see before.

Have you ever looked at one of the *magic eye* pictures? These are pictures in which, from a casual glance, you see one obvious scene or design. Yet when you refocus and train your perception, you see an entirely different picture within the picture. This is similar to the skill of noticing we want to develop. For example, the earlier activity of writing down ten things you were thankful for illustrates this. I'm guessing that you didn't even notice those things you were thankful for when you started your day. It wasn't until you paused to think about it that you realized the many things you have to be thankful for.

So you'll be further developing your skill of noticing throughout your thirty-one mini- adventures. You'll also be developing the skill of savoring. When we savor something, we take the time to enjoy it for as long as possible. We appreciate, relish, and bask in it. Whether it's a feeling of joy or a piece of chocolate cake, when you savor something, you enjoy it to the fullest. You enjoy it so much that you want to make it last forever. With that in mind, savoring carries a connotation of doing something slowly. If you savor that warm piece of pecan pie, you eat it slowly, bit by bit, deliberately picking every last crumb off the plate. The word is often applied to eating, but you can savor any pleasurable experience, whether it's a cozy fireplace, your child's smile, or a friend's compliment.

In summary, to savor is to enjoy something fully. So why don't we do that more often? If an experience is so enjoyable, wouldn't we naturally want to stop and enjoy it for a while?

For one thing, we aren't in the habit. Instead, we're in the habit of being busy and rushing, which precludes slowing down to savor. Our *to do* list is our priority; our lifestyle is like a hamster wheel on which we keep spinning around. In order to become more joyful and content, we're going to have to decide that it's worth it sometimes to slow down and savor—to enjoy something for a while.

We have some great models of this in the Psalms. For example, notice how David slows down and ponders little by little some of the wonderful things about God:

> On the glorious splendor of Your majesty
> And on Your wonderful works, I will meditate.
> Men shall speak of the power of Your awesome acts,
> And I will tell of Your greatness.

> They shall eagerly utter the memory of Your abundant goodness, And will shout joyfully of Your righteousness.
> The LORD is gracious and merciful;
> Slow to anger and great in lovingkindness.
> The LORD is good to all, And His mercies are over all His works (Ps. 145:5–9 NASB).

David goes on at length, savoring God's goodness and glory. This is true in so many other psalms that relish God's spectacular attributes. The Scripture writers also set an example of savoring the beauty all around us in creation:

> He makes springs pour water into the ravines; it flows between the mountains.
> They give water to all the beasts of the field; the wild donkeys quench their thirst.
> The birds of the air nest by the waters; they sing among the branches.
> He waters the mountains from his upper chambers; the earth is satisfied by the fruit of his work. He makes grass grow for the cattle, and plants for man to cultivate –
> bringing forth food from the earth: wine that gladdens the heart of man, oil to make his face shine, and bread that sustains his heart.
> The trees of the LORD are well watered, the cedars of Lebanon that he planted.
> There the birds make their nests; the stork has its home in the pine trees (Ps. 104:10–17 NIV).

In these sentences, the writer is noticing and savoring the many details of nature all around him.

At the beginning of each week's mini-adventures, you'll have a portion of Scripture to notice and savor. You'll see that I've given you some general questions to help you develop these skills, while thinking about the verses and applying their truths to yourself. Marinating (so to speak) in these biblical thoughts will prepare you to launch into your particular adventures for that week.

So it's time to jump in; notice, savor, and have fun!

Questions to Ponder and Discuss

- Reflect back over your lists of ten items that you were thankful for. Talk about this activity with someone who crosses your path this week.
- What are your greatest hindrances to developing the habit of noticing and savoring good things around you? The busyness of your schedule? Difficulty in seeing this as a priority? Identifying your obstacles is the first step toward overcoming them.
- What advantages do you see for yourself in developing the habit of noticing and savoring?
- In the previous passages, Psalm 145:5–9 and Psalm 104:10–17, underline and discuss the various things the writers notice and savor. Which of these are especially meaningful or noteworthy to you?

Notes

Week 1

Prepare Your Heart and Mind

Prepare yourself for this week's adventures by reading the following passage. Before you begin, pray that God will speak to you as you think about these verses. Underline words and phrases that express to you joy, positivity, and well-being. Read the passage again, and write down any changes you'd like to see in your life based upon these verses. Read it one more time, jotting down any other observations, comments, questions, or applications that come to mind. Use this book or your journal to record your thoughts.

> Rejoice in the Lord always. I will say it again: Rejoice! Let your gentleness be evident to all. The Lord is near. Do not be anxious about anything, but in every situation, by prayer and petition, with thanksgiving, present your requests to God. And the peace of God, which transcends all understanding, will guard your hearts and your minds in Christ Jesus. Finally, brothers and sisters, whatever is true, whatever is noble, whatever is right, whatever is pure, whatever is lovely, whatever is admirable—if anything is excellent or praiseworthy—think about such things. Whatever you have learned or received or heard from me, or seen in me—put it into practice. And the God of peace will be with you (Phil. 4:4–8 NIV).

Notes

Day 1: Count Your Many Blessings

> Finally, brethren, whatever is true, whatever is honorable, whatever is right, whatever is pure, whatever is lovely, whatever is of good repute, if there is any excellence and if anything worthy of praise, dwell on these things (Phil. 4:8 NASB).

Every day, a steady stream of good things passes you by, unnoticed and un-savored. If noticed and savored, your moments can be infused with increasing joy, wonder, and appreciation. From sunny weather to kind, complimentary words to a friendly email to flowers along the freeway to a favorite song to a new spiritual insight to a job accomplishment—there are numerous opportunities in each day to lift mundane or gloomy existence to radiant new levels. Today, notice each thing that brings you a spark of joy or a surge of happiness. Write it here or in your specially-purchased notebook or journal, and enjoy. Then, at the end of the day as you lay your head on the pillow, savor each individual blessing. For an extra portion of joy, start the next day looking over them again.

Create a lifelong habit. As you lay your head on your pillow each night, reflect back over your day and savor at least three happy moments from that day.

Notes

Day 2: Beauty Quest

> Every good thing given and every perfect gift is from above, coming down from the Father of lights, with whom there is no variation or shifting shadow (James 1:17 NASB).

John Keats wrote, "A thing of beauty is a joy forever." Beauty is everywhere: in the blue sky outside your window, in flowers that dot the freeway landscape, in the patterns on a garden lizard's back, in the kindness of a face, in the artwork displayed on your wall. Yet, how often do we bustle through the day without noting it. Today, make a point of noticing, writing down, and mentally savoring each item of beauty that crosses your path. You may be surprised at how much there is to enjoy that you've never noticed before. Then, savor your sightings by looking back over what you've written at the day's end.

Notes

Day 3: Notice What You Do Well

> I will give thanks to You, for I am fearfully and wonderfully made; Wonderful are Your works, and my soul knows it very well (Ps. 139:14 NASB).

Every person is a unique creation of God—His masterpiece. You are a unique creation of God; you are His masterpiece. Like every snowflake, each human being is distinctly different. God has imbued you with unique strengths, qualities, perspectives, and talents.

Throughout this day, notice these things about yourself, and rejoice in them. Whether it's your sense of humor, the warmth you convey in a phone conversation, your professional talent, your musical ability, or your logical thinking, notice, savor, give thanks, and write down each thing throughout the day. Below is a list of ideas to get you started.

- creativity
- people skills
- academic ability
- athletic ability
- love for God
- sense of humor
- job skills and gifting
- appreciation of beauty
- analytical ability
- love for people
- character qualities
- positivity

Notes

Day 4: Good News!

> Like cold water to a weary soul, so is good news from a distant land (Prov. 25:25 NASB).

Good news is everywhere if you look for it. Positive, unexpected things happen to you, both small and large. You hear good news about a friend, you receive an unexpected email, or something pleasant happens in your family or community. Amazingly, good news can even be found on television or in the newspaper! Throughout this day, make it your goal to notice good news: positive information that you didn't previously know. And remember, nothing is too small to rejoice about. When possible, tell someone. And of course, record each item in your journal to enhance your joy.

Notes

Day 5: Best Memories of Your Life

> However many years a man may live, let him enjoy them all (Eccl. 11:8 NIV).

Keep it simple: Sometimes we rob ourselves of joy by making things too complex. Keep each of your thirty-one adventures simple and easy-going. For example, if this is a busy day for you, choose only two or three of your life memories to think about. And you need only think about each one for two or three minutes if that works best for you. Simplicity clears the way for joy to bloom.

Jump into your mental time machine today and relive some of your best memories. Turn your dial to scan your childhood, teen years, young adulthood, early marriage, parenting, and beyond. Think of school memories, holidays, special relationships, and outdoor experiences. For today, select three to five of them, and re-experience them through your five senses. Put yourself back into each memory and think about what you saw, heard, felt, tasted, and smelled. Then add a sixth sense: your emotional feelings. Think of positive words that describe your feelings in that memory: open, happy, alive, loved, respected, empathetic, awed, enthusiastic, zealous, courageous, inspired, or admired. Bathe in those feelings for a moment.

You don't have to stop everything to savor a memory. You can do this while you're cooking, getting ready in the morning, waiting, driving, or eating. You can take a two-minute mental break from a task for a moment of reflection. You can even talk about it with a friend or co-worker. Then invite that person to share a memory with you in this same way, and double your pleasure, double your fun!

Notes

Week 2

A Lifestyle of Joy: Principle 2— Can You Say Neuroplasticity?

Neuroplasticity has become an exciting word in science this past decade. Simply put, it means that our brains physically change with our new experiences and the new things that we learn. This means that our experiences and growth can literally rewire our brains. It was formerly thought that our brains physically stayed the same throughout our lives.

Science now believes that our brains actually change physically with repeated experiences and repeated thought patterns. This is exciting because it means that we are not stuck in a rut with the brains we've been given. Our brains change and rewire themselves based upon what we do, think, and choose.

For example, think of an old farm road that's been muddy in the past, and now there are deep, solid grooves from where trucks and cars have driven. As a result, when you drive your car on that road, your tires automatically go into those deep grooves, forcing you to drive on the well-worn path. But let's say it rains again and the ground is soft and mushy. Now when you drive on this road, you form new grooves and don't have to automatically follow the ruts that were formerly there. Neuroplasticity is like this. When you learn new things and have new experiences, your physical brain can be changed, reshaped, and rewired, making it easier for your thoughts and emotions to go down new pathways instead of being stuck in their old ways. Is this perhaps what happens in the process of Romans 12:2?

> And do not be conformed to this world, but be transformed by the renewing of your mind (Romans 12:2 NASB).

As our minds are renewed by the new spiritual experiences and information we give them, our brains are literally transformed and renewed physically.

This is such encouraging news in our mini-adventures. The new habits we're forming are physically rewiring our brains, according to science. You're creating a new you!

This can all be explained in scientific terminology about synapses and neural pathways and axonal sprouting. There's a lot of information about this topic on the Internet if you want to look it up. In simpler terms, let's think of an example we can relate to from daily life: the example of dyeing our hair.

It's as if, as we dyed our hair over and over, the genetic marker for the hair color itself was gradually being changed. Therefore, we wouldn't have to work hard re-dyeing it over and over again. It would gradually be permanently changed to the new color.

That's what scientists are discovering our brains have been created to do. This is motivating when it comes to being consistent on our mini-adventures each day and with other habitual spiritual and emotional practices. You're transforming your brain, so it won't always take so much work to implement your new habits—they become a part of who you are. For example, the skills of noticing and savoring that we talked about in the last chapter can become an automatic part of who you are, along with other positive, joyful ways of being.

When I think of my own life, this has been true in the area of food. As a teenager and young adult, I found my mind occupied throughout each day with thoughts of food and my weight. I know that many people can identify with this. I was either looking forward eagerly to my next meal or anguishing about how much I'd eaten that day, obsessing about my weight. It was a vicious cycle that I tried to break for a long time without success until I enrolled in a program that retrained my brain and its automatic thought processes. The program involved tuning into the body's natural hunger cycles, eating only when truly physically hungry, and stopping eating when naturally full, not stuffed. Eventually, after fighting my old, embedded patterns of thought and behavior for a period of time, I can honestly say that my physical body is rewired with a different, natural rhythm. What started with consistent mental effort has become a physically-driven process, and I can experience the peaceful, enjoyable process of food intake without my former anxiety and turmoil.

Something many of us can identify with is the example of riding a bike or driving a car. When we first started learning these skills, it took a great deal of mental effort to remember each step and action. After practicing them repeatedly over time, you eventually did the necessary actions without any conscious thought. Science says that this is neuroplasticity; our physical brains have undergone a physical change. New grooves have been formed that thoughts naturally flow along without any conscious effort.

In this week's activities, you'll have the opportunity to rewire your brain through physical, emotional, and spiritual avenues. Let neuroplasticity have its way on your playful, creative, daily adventures.

Questions to Ponder and Discuss

- When you think of the example of the farm road and negative ruts that your brain automatically follows, can you identify one or two negative patterns that you easily fall into?
- What people or life experiences trained you in negative or critical thought patterns?
- Can you think of examples from your life in which your brain has already formed new, healthier, more positive patterns? If not, then you're in the right place for experiencing this transformation.

Notes

Week Two

Prepare Your Heart and Mind

Prepare yourself for this week's adventures by reading the following passage. Before you begin, pray that God will speak to you as you think about these verses. Underline words and phrases that express to you joy, positivity, and well-being. Read the passage again, and write down any changes you'd like to see in your life based upon these verses. Read it one more time, jotting down any other observations, comments, questions, or applications that come to mind. Use this book or your journal to record your thoughts.

And Mary said:

> "My soul glorifies the Lord and my spirit rejoices in God my Savior, for he has been mindful of the humble state of his servant. From now on all generations will call me blessed, for the Mighty One has done great things for me—holy is his name. His mercy extends to those who fear him, from generation to generation. He has performed mighty deeds with his arm; he has scattered those who are proud in their inmost thoughts. He has brought down rulers from their thrones but has lifted up the humble. He has filled the hungry with good things but has sent the rich away empty. He has helped his servant Israel, remembering to be merciful to Abraham and his descendants forever, just as he promised our ancestors" (Luke 1:46–55 NIV).

Notes

Day 6: Opposite Day

> I would have despaired unless I had believed that I would see the goodness of the Lord in the land of the living (Ps. 27:13 NASB).

Today, any time you catch yourself thinking a negative thought about a person, situation, or anything else, immediately state an opposite, positive perspective about it. Try to say it out loud or, at least, form a complete mental sentence about it. For example, if you're discouraged because you make a mistake or fail at something, you might tell yourself, *Everyone makes mistakes. Everyone will make countless mistakes in a lifetime. I'm going to learn from this, leave it behind, and not waste any more energy worrying about it!* Or, if you find yourself worrying about your finances, you might choose the thought, *I'm glad that God is in control of everything, and He is going to work this out.* If you have a bad attitude about a co-worker or family member, you could think, *I want the best for that person, and hope that they find success and fulfillment.* (You could even pray this for them at that moment.) Don't try to justify your positive thought or think about details of how it will work out; simply retrain your brain to think the positive and to see possibilities rather than problems.

Your written note about this can be as simple as, "Finances: God has worked it out in the past. He is in control." Or "Tom: hard worker and sense of humor." Of course, write more fully if you like.

Notes

Day 7: Smile!

Bright eyes gladden the heart (Prov. 15:30 NASB).

Your goal today is simple: smile as many times as possible. Numerous studies have shown that people experience positive emotion simply by holding their mouths in a smiling position. It seems that involuntary biological changes occur as a result of this positioning of one's facial muscles. Research reveals that smiling releases endorphins, natural pain killers, and serotonin. Together, these biochemicals make us feel good. Smiling is a natural drug.

Put smiley-face stick-up notes where you'll see them throughout the day. Then, smile, smile, smile! Look for opportunities when you're experiencing authentic positivity, and express it fully upon your face. Think about letting the smile and its emotion spread throughout your body, from your head down your neck through your torso and into your arms and legs, like a warm glow flowing throughout. Even laugh whenever possible.

Also, notice the smiles and friendly faces you encounter throughout this day. Notice and savor them.

You might be surprised at how your joy will be boosted by the smiles you experience throughout today's journey.

Notes

Day 8: Doors Close, New Doors Open

> Weeping may last for the night, but a shout of joy comes in the morning (Ps. 30:5 NASB).

There's a sneaky pattern of life that you may miss if you don't look for it. When one door closes it's often followed by another one opening.

Life's journey involves closed doors: opportunities are denied, health declines, relationships end, geographical moves are required. Like a magnet, these events can pull our attention to dwell on the negative aspects of these situations. But for those who will look and notice, closed doors often result in new doors that wouldn't have opened otherwise. Without conscious attention, we often don't realize that, without the closed door, the next door wouldn't have opened. For example, a job loss eventually means a new career is found, a relational difficulty means that new relationships are formed or life lessons are learned, and a health difficultly may result in healthier lifestyle choices or a new life direction.

Throughout this day, reflect back on your life to notice this closed door/open door pattern. To get your brain going, think of major life events, changes, disappointments, health issues, dreams denied, and even small daily events. Also, if something disappointing happens today, notice if it provides an opportunity for something good to follow. You have to wait in line, but you get to talk someone else who's waiting. They're out of your favorite snack at your coffee place, but you get to try something new. You receive some frustrating news, but it enables you to bond with someone as you tell him/her about it.

When you look behind a dark cloud, you'll often become aware of both a silver lining and a promising new horizon.

Write here or in your journal about each closed door/open door that you think of.

Notes

Day 9: God Sightings

He who has ears to hear, let him hear (Matt. 11:15 NASB).

God is at work everywhere, all the time... have you noticed? He's working in

- people around us
- our own thoughts
- our own hearts
- events around us
- our surroundings
- answered prayers
- local, state, national, and world events

Are you regularly tuned in to His frequency? Have you put on your 4-D glasses to be able to perceive His activities? If you're not seeing Him work, then guess who isn't working? You! You're not doing your work of watching and noticing.

Today, your adventure involves proactively being on the lookout for God's hands at work, or His fingerprints indicating where He has been. You might notice things like:

- A conversation *just happens* where you are able to meet someone's needs, or they meet yours.
- You have been experiencing a growing dissatisfaction with something about yourself.
- You realize that God is prompting you to grow and change.
- When you hear or read about local, national, or global events, you stop and ask God about His part or plans in these events.

- You start or continue to pray for something or someone, and you watch to see increments of change. You notice and thank God for even small changes, also realizing that *wait* and *no* are answers from God's infinite wisdom, worthy of thanksgiving and trust.
- You feel prompted inwardly to say something (or not to say something) to someone, and you follow this prompting.
- You're continually on the lookout for where God is working, and how He wants you to join Him in that work.

Today, fine-tune your spiritual antenna to pick up *God sightings.* You could write each of the bulleted categories in the first list above on a note card to carry with you (people around us, our own thoughts, our own hearts, etc.), and ask God right now to help you notice His workings today. Then converse with Him about each sighting, thanking and praising Him along the way.

It's amazing what you see when you're looking through a spiritual lens. So pray, and then go through your day looking and listening.

Notes

Day 10: Give, Give, and Give Again

> Each one must do just as he has purposed in his heart, not grudgingly or under compulsion, for God loves a cheerful giver (2 Cor. 9:7 NASB).

On today's adventure, you'll be a sleuth on the lookout for ways to give—through words, actions, prayer, or even money.

There's great joy to be found in giving; happiness is the natural by-product. As people cross your mind or path today, think of little ways you might give to them: a compliment, an encouraging note or email, a phone call to see how they're doing. If you eat out, maybe give a little extra tip. You might anonymously give someone ten dollars, twenty dollars, or more, just for fun! If a child is in your life, make him or her feel special with words or actions. If you see someone needing help, step in and give of yourself. You might be surprised at how happy giving makes you feel. Remember the words of the Lord Jesus,"It is more blessed to give than to receive" (Acts 20:35 NIV).

Notes

Week 3

A Lifestyle of Joy: Principle 3—Out with the Old, In with the New

So is it really that simple? We just need to program new, positive things into our brains and we'll be new, happier people?

If you try that for any length of time, you'll discover that you need a more multifaceted approach, as is the case with most of life's challenges. Think of it like a pie cut into different-sized pieces—a pie graph. One piece of the joyfulness pie is retraining your brain through new habits like the thirty-one adventures. Other pieces involve tending to our spiritual, relational, and physical needs. Another piece involves understanding the roots of your unique, individual negative thought patterns. When you understand the roots better, you can apply specifically-designed solutions to address these problematic areas.

We've all developed negative habits in our thoughts and feelings from past experiences with people around us and things we've gone through. If the people we grew up with looked at life through a negative lens or were habitually critical or complaining, we probably picked up unhealthy patterns. If we had unusual hardship growing up, it probably trained our minds in negative ways.

Justin's mother was often critical of him when he was a child, disciplining him harshly. Consequently, Justin subconsciously carried certain internal messages about himself into most of his adult experiences. Two of his default negative messages were, *I don't deserve love* and *I am shameful*. These messages affected him for many years in both relationships and employment situations, often being expressed as insecurity and anger. As Justin became aware of these lenses, he started to learn more accurate, objective ways to look at himself and situations. In this process, he gained more inner freedom, lightheartedness, and joy.

Throughout my years of counseling, I've discovered that we all have subconscious messages about ourselves that are inaccurate or downright lies. As people become aware of and replace these automatic thoughts with more accurate perspectives, they find that they're set free and enjoy life and relationships far more. The following are a few of the most common faulty self-perceptions and their opposing, more accurate self-statements.

Faulty Thinking	**Accurate Thinking**
I don't deserve love.	I can have love; I am loved.
I am a bad person.	I am righteous in Christ.
I am worthless.	I have great worth.
I am shameful.	I am honorable.
I am not good enough.	Christ has given me great worth and value.
I cannot succeed.	I can succeed.
I am powerless.	I have choices and options.
I cannot protect myself.	I can protect myself.
I am stupid.	I have intelligence.
I am insignificant (unimportant).	God has given me significance.
I am a disappointment.	I am fine the way God has made me.
I am a failure.	I can succeed.
I have to be perfect.	I can be myself.
I am permanently damaged.	I can be healthy.
I am ugly.	I am fine the way God has made me.
I should have done something different.	I did the best I could.
I am in danger.	It's over; I am safe now.
I cannot stand it.	I can handle it with God's help.
I am not safe.	I am safe now.
It's my fault.	It's not my fault.
I'm broken.	I'm beginning to heal; I am whole in Christ.
I am inferior.	God has given me great worth and strengths.

As you look at the statements above in the column on the left, which of these faulty self-statements might be applicable to you in certain circumstances? As you look at the column on the right, consider for a few moments how each corresponding accurate statement directly opposes your faulty thinking. You can utilize this process of replacing your negative thoughts about yourself with positive ones as you journey through different experiences. Through practice, you'll come to quickly identify times when you believe lies about yourself; then, you'll be able to retrain your brain to see yourself through an accurate lens.

An example of this occurred in a recent group meeting when I was with several colleagues and our directors. I asked a question, and one of the directors responded to me in a way that made me feel belittled and unintelligent. I immediately felt ashamed and didn't speak for the rest of the meeting. Thoughts of this interaction continued to plague me over the following days, and I finally discussed it with one of my friends, also a counselor. As we talked, I realized that the feeling I was having was exactly like what I felt many times as a child when my mom would treat me in negative ways. As an adult, this made me especially vulnerable to feeling that *I am inferior* and *I did something wrong.* As a child, my response was to withdraw and cower in fear—a reaction that as an adult, I could inadvertently re-experience in subtle, yet powerful ways. Talking to my friend about the meeting, I realized that I was once more replicating this thought and behavior pattern. In a way, the director at the meeting had become my mother, and I was the shamed child. In realizing this, I also realized that I'm no longer that child; I now have a variety of options and perspectives that I lacked then. As opposed to thinking that I'm inferior, today I know that God has given me great worth and my own strengths, one of which is intelligence. As opposed to thinking, *I did something wrong,* I realized that in this situation, I didn't do anything wrong by asking my question. In fact, I'd asked an insightful question, and I'd either misinterpreted the director's response, or her harsh reply had been a result of her own issues.

As a result of this thought process, I made an appointment with the director and discussed our interaction in an honest, healthy way. She had been totally unaware of the way she'd come across, apologized, and affirmed the validity and importance of what I'd asked. It strengthened our relationship, both then and for the months ahead. It also strengthened me to live in truths about myself rather than lies.

This example demonstrates how our inaccurate thought patterns keep us from experiencing joy and well-being, while counteracting them to establish new thought patterns sets us free. As we go through the mental process of replacing the lies we've believed with truths about ourselves, the result is increasing joy and strength. Many verses and passages in the Bible contain these positive truths about us. As you memorize and meditate upon these, you'll experience powerful transformation. The following are a few examples:

> I will give thanks to you because I have been so amazingly and miraculously made. Your works are miraculous, and my soul is fully aware of this (Ps. 139:14 GWT).

> For we are God's masterpiece. He has created us anew in Christ Jesus, so we can do the good things he planned for us long ago (Eph. 2:10 NLT).

> I have loved you with an everlasting love; Therefore I have drawn you with lovingkindness (Jer. 31:3 NASB).

Building a strong foundation of truth within yourself, about yourself, is an important aspect of living the joy-filled life that God desires for you. This is an overflowing life because, as you experience it within yourself, you can't help but positively impact people around you. In this way, greater and greater joy will abound.

Questions to Ponder and Discuss

- In the list of *Faulty Thinking* sentences in this chapter, which negative self – statements are you vulnerable to believing about yourself? In your upbringing or past experiences, how were these negative perspectives created and reinforced within you?
- In the corresponding list of *Accurate Thinking* sentences, which statements counteract your negative self-statements?

What objective evidence do you have that these positive self-statements are true?

- What Bible verses support your answers to the second question?
- Can you think of an experience in your life in which you automatically believed a negative self-statement about yourself? What would have been a more accurate, objective, positive truth about yourself in that situation? What evidence or Bible verse supports this positive perspective about yourself?

Notes

Week Three

Prepare Your Heart and Mind

Prepare yourself for this week's adventures by reading the following passage. Before you begin, pray that God will speak to you as you think about these verses. Underline words and phrases that express to you joy, positivity, and well-being. Read the passage again, and write down any changes you'd like to see in your life based upon these verses. Read it one more time, jotting down any other observations, comments, questions, or applications that come to mind. Use this book or your journal to record your thoughts.

> Praise be to the God and Father of our Lord Jesus Christ, who has blessed us in the heavenly realms with every spiritual blessing in Christ. For he chose us in him before the creation of the world to be holy and blameless in his sight. In love he predestined us for adoption to sonship through Jesus Christ, in accordance with his pleasure and will—to the praise of his glorious grace, which he has freely given us in the One he loves. In him we have redemption through his blood, the forgiveness of sins, in accordance with the riches of God's grace that he lavished on us. With all wisdom and understanding, he made known to us the mystery of his will according to his good pleasure, which he purposed in Christ, to be put into effect when the times reach their fulfillment—to bring unity to all things in heaven and on earth under Christ. In him we were also chosen, having been predestined according to the plan of him who works out everything in conformity with the purpose of his will, in order that we, who were the first to put our

hope in Christ, might be for the praise of his glory. And you also were included in Christ when you heard the message of truth, the gospel of your salvation. When you believed, you were marked in him with a seal, the promised Holy Spirit, who is a deposit guaranteeing our inheritance until the redemption of those who are God's possession—to the praise of his glory. For this reason, ever since I heard about your faith in the Lord Jesus and your love for all God's people, I have not stopped giving thanks for you, remembering you in my prayers (Eph. 1:3–16 NIV).

Notes

Day 11: Appreciate God Through the ABCs

> On the glorious splendor of Your majesty, And on Your wonderful works, I will meditate (Ps.145:5 NASB).

Close your eyes and call to mind a stunning scene in nature or a moving artistic endeavor you've experienced: a glorious sunset, lush greenery, an awe-inspiring musical or stage performance. Stop right now, visualize it in your mind, and place yourself there. What's your emotional response? Warmth? Joy? Excitement? These same emotions can well up when we perceive the various facets of God's being with our spiritual senses. And yet, this usually doesn't happen automatically; we have to consciously *turn on* our spiritual senses throughout our day-to-day experience of Him.

> Perfectionism is a robber of joy. You don't have to be perfect on these thirty-one adventures. If you try to be, it may sabotage your very goal of gladness. For example, if you only get halfway through the alphabet today, rejoice that you accomplished so much in thinking about God. If you forget to do an activity one day, don't beat yourself up; just do it the next day. Your goal is learning new ways to experience joy, not perfection.

Today's exercise will teach you to strengthen this habit of perceiving and enjoying God's wonderful personhood. As you go through your moments today, call to mind characteristics of God by working your way through the alphabet, and contemplate each characteristic for a moment. For example:

8:00 am: *A,* Lord, I love the way You are all-knowing. You are so wise and intelligent, knowing everything about every person and every subject.

8:05 am: *B,* Lord, You are big! You are everywhere, and You created the universe. You make me feel such worth that someone so magnificent loves and cares about me!

9:10 am: *C*, God, I love Your creativity. You thought up the duckbilled platypus, lightning, and the planets. You invented colors out of nothing.

Enjoy His qualities throughout the day, as you meditate upon this wonderful God who loves and cares about you so much.

Notes

Day 12: Delight in Your Day

But Mary treasured all these things, pondering them in her heart (Luke 2:19 NASB).

When we treasure something, we value and take pleasure in it. This is similar to savoring, which involves dwelling upon something with delight. *Treasuring* and *savoring* are important skills that can infuse your life with greater joy. Today, you'll practice and develop these skills.

Your goal is to notice and proactively savor and treasure the positive experiences of your day, both small and large. A key to this is thinking through each of your five senses at any given moment (sight, hearing, touch, smell, and taste) and lingering upon any enjoyment you feel. For example, when you look out your window to enjoy the sunny weather or the cleansing rain, drink in the experience by focusing on each of your senses to fully become aware. Linger on what your eyes see, what your skin feels in terms of warmth, coolness, or pleasure, and what you smell and hear. Treasure the tastes that cross your palate today; don't just chew and swallow—dwell on them with delight. You might need your reminder method to keep you alert to positive things that come along: a rubber band on your wrist, a small symbol on your hand in ink, or a special piece of jewelry. Write down each item, pausing to cherish, value, and enjoy. You are savoring and treasuring. Here's part of one person's list:

1. When I walked into the kitchen this morning, I savored the smell of fresh coffee brewing. When I tasted it, I specifically focused on how good it was.
2. My cat rubbed against my leg, and I was aware of the softness of her fur against my skin. When I reached down to pet her, I dwelt upon how soft her fur was and the endearing nature of her purr.

3. I realized at work how much I love the atmosphere of our office. The artwork has been carefully chosen, and I made a point of looking at it and appreciating it. I drank in the warm, calm environment of the hallway and the enjoyable laughter coming from a room down the hall. I paused inwardly just to appreciate it all for a few moments.
4. In the copy room at work, a co-worker commented on the attractiveness of my suit. I felt good about that, and back in my office, I enjoyed the sight and feel of my suit, savoring the compliment and enjoying the feeling of pride in my appearance.

So you get the idea. Now go drink in your day. Hear, see, smell, taste, touch — savor, treasure, and enjoy!

Notes

Day 13: The Strengths of My People

> I thank my God in all my remembrance of you (Phil. 1:3 NASB).

Have you ever watched a movie and felt inwardly changed by one of the characters? You might have learned something to apply to an area of your life, whether marriage or parenting or some area of struggle. Or maybe you felt fired up to go out and replicate a character's example in your own sphere of influence.

All around us, people are living out their strengths. Today, think through the significant people in your life, and mentally list their strengths. Remember specific situations where you've witnessed their strengths in action. Be sure to include family, friends, and co-workers. One way to do this is to think of a different person every couple of hours or right after each meal or snack. Spread your positivity throughout the day. And if you're tempted to compare yourself and feel *less* than those you're thinking of, look back at Day 3 to remember the strengths God has given you. Then return to your mental celebration of the people in your life.

Notes

Day 14: Statements of Self-Esteem

> God created man in His own image, in the image of God He created him;male and female He created them (Gen. 1:27 NASB).

King David, Israel's greatest ruler, exclaimed exuberantly in one of his writings,

> What is man that You take thought of him,
> And the Son of Man that You care for him?
> Yet You have made him a little lower than God,
> And You crown him with glory and majesty!"
> (Ps. 8:4–5 NASB).

Our lives can be filled with a deep sense of joy and contentment when we build our foundational thoughts about ourselves upon the many amazing, positive perspectives that are true. Too often, however, our thoughts are pulled magnetically to the faulty beliefs and values of our culture that base an individual's worth upon temporal surface traits, such as appearance, wealth, or achievement. When we attach our sense of value to these things, our emotions will be driven and tossed like a kite in the wind of fickle human perspective. It's important to enjoy and value the strengths and gifts we've been given, but we also need to build within ourselves a firm foundation based upon our true value and worth. Continuing joy will be the result.

Today, you'll be strengthening this foundation by filling your mind with positive truths about yourself. Review the list below several times today. Write it on a card, photocopy it, or carry this book with you. Read it silently or aloud, thinking about the truths inherent in each statement. In this way, you'll be thinking about yourself as God does, and experiencing His joy along the way.

1. God created me in His image. I am His masterpiece (Genesis 1:27).
2. God paid the highest price for me. He gave His Son so that I can live with Him forever. The fact that the highest price was paid for me reflects the great worth that God has given me (John 3:16).
3. Because I have accepted Jesus as my Savior, God has completely forgiven me for everything I've ever done wrong, and everything I ever will do wrong (Col. 2:13–14).
4. Because I have accepted Jesus as my Savior, God now sees me as completely righteous and blameless (Col. 1:21–22).
5. I can enjoy being a one-of-a-kind portrait. Just as no two snowflakes are exactly alike, there's no other person like me. I can enjoy being unique.
6. I have unique gifts and strengths. I can grow in my awareness and enjoyment of them.
7. I am God's masterpiece, created to do good things that He has planned for me (Eph. 2:10).
8. I value myself highly because God does.
9. When I'm criticized by others, this in no way reflects upon or diminishes my worth or value.
10. I can notice and enjoy each sign of my own achievement or progress, no matter how insignificant it may seem to me or others.
11. I can enjoy the achievements and progress that others make, without concluding they're more valuable than I am as a person.
12. I'm deeply cherished and treasured by the King of the universe (John 17:23b).

Notes

Day 15: Live in the Moment

> Therefore do not worry about tomorrow, for tomorrow will worry about itself. Each day has enough trouble of its own (Matthew 6:34 NIV).

To live in the moment means to be conscious, to be aware, and to be in the present with all of your senses. It means to immerse yourself in life, discovering the meaning, joy, and beauty in each experience—not wasting energy on past or future moments. It means not thinking about or dwelling on the past, nor being anxious or worrying about the future. When we give our attention to the present, we give our full attention to what we're doing and experiencing in real time. We embrace everything we do and every person we encounter with our full attention. Even when resting, we peacefully savor the moment. It gives us the opportunity to recharge, renew, and gain clarity.

Today, you're going to practice this skill at various times. You'll be training your mind to focus on your current activity. Try each of the following practices a couple of times today, engaging attentively in what you're doing, and enjoying the process. (Write these on a card as a reminder, especially if this is a new concept for you.)

- Peacefully notice your surroundings for several moments—sights, sounds, ambiance, and people.
- Think specifically about each of your five senses, and one-by-one, enjoy what they're experiencing: sight, hearing, smell, taste, and touch.
- Listen attentively to words being spoken, music, or even silence.
- Savor your food and drink. Taste each morsel.

So enjoy your day, intentionally focusing upon living in the moment. Treasure your moments; treasure your life.

Notes

Week 4

A Lifestyle of Joy: Principal 4— Joy-Robbers, Part One

You walk through your front door and are sickened by the scene. Your home has been ravaged by a thief. Cabinet doors hang open, their contents strewn about the floor. Books have been thrown off shelves, and they now lay carelessly open, some of their pages torn. In your bedroom, your drawers have been invaded and personal items inspected. Some beloved framed pictures have been thrown to the ground, damaged by shattered glass. You eventually discover that some treasured personal items have been stolen that can never be replaced, not to mention more expensive objects that will not be repurchased easily.

"The thief comes only to steal and kill and destroy; I came that they may have life, and have it abundantly" (John 10:10 NASB). Jesus described very well what we might experience if our homes were ravaged by a thief. The words *steal*, *kill* and *destroy* carry heavy emotional connotations. These words also describe what happens when we allow things into our lives that rob us of joy and well-being. Often without realizing it, we allow certain culprits to steal and kill and destroy us from within. In contrast, the second part of Jesus' statement describes what God desires for each of us: the experience of inner abundance—a life overflowing with joy, peace, love, etc. (Galatians 5:22). However, in order to experience these things, we have to prevent thieves from coming in, or kick them out if they're already inside.

Many centuries ago, King Solomon wrote, "Catch the foxes for us, the little foxes that are ruining the vineyards, while our vineyards are in blossom" (Song 2:15 NASB). Think about that picture: rows and rows of healthy green vines with their beautiful leaves and luscious grapes. Then, little foxes come into them; maybe they're even cute and winsome little foxes. They slowly, stealthily start eating grapes and damaging vines. As a result, the foxes get bigger and eat more. It doesn't take long for them to fatten into big foxes that are well-fed and nourished. Ultimately, they take over the vineyard and start running things their way.

This is what can happen in our lives, but with a different kind of fox, a different kind of thief. These different thieves come in stealthily, subtly, seemingly attractive at first, but they eventually wreak havoc with our inner well-being. So in this chapter and the next, let's think about some of the most common joy-robbers so that you can banish them from your vineyard as you're welcoming in new, life-giving habits.

Keeping Your Schedule Too Intense

An overly intense life will steal your joy quickly. By this I mean either keeping your schedule too full or having too many events or people in your day or week that require excessive energy. You may have already started learning this on your own, but to add fuel to my argument, let me point out a few interesting factors. It's significant that in Genesis, chapters one and two, God demonstrated a pattern and revealed a priority of setting aside one–seventh of each week for resting. Prioritizing rest in this way can be foreign to our way of thinking and living. In addition to this weekly pattern, God designed us so that approximately one-third of each day we do nothing but sleep. This fact reveals that God has a very different priority for intensity and activity than we do. To add further evidence for my case, Jesus was only in public ministry for three out of his thirty-three years on this planet. By our modern standard, if we had placed the Son of God on this earth, we would have had Him working publicly by the age of twenty and not leaving the planet until at least seventy or eighty years of age. Aren't we supposed to squeeze the most out of every opportunity that we can? Yet by these examples, we see that intensity and excessive activity are *not* high priorities for our wise, divine designer. We would do well to follow His example.

A couple of weeks ago, I had a day filled with my favorite activities. I love my work of counseling people, and I love performing in improv shows. On that particular Monday, from 9:00 am until 10:00 pm, I got to do both of these activities. But the previous week had also been full of nonstop activity, and the following week would be the same. So on that Monday, instead of enjoying the things I love to do, I experienced tiredness and drudgery. This is an example of what I'm talking about; even the things we love aren't fun when we allow our lives to be too intense.

Allowing Our Emotional, Spiritual, or Physical Reservoir to Get Too Low

This is a common joy-robber. Picture a full reservoir: a vast expanse of life-giving water, ready to provide its replenishing abundance whenever other resources run dry. Ideally, reservoirs are kept full so that plenty of water can be provided if needed. This is because, if a drought is significant and there isn't enough water, things will either suffer, wither, or die.

You and I are like that. We have to keep our internal reservoirs full emotionally, spiritually, and physically because each of these is continually being drained in small and large ways. We have to learn about and monitor ourselves, knowing what replenishes our energy and what drains our energy, and how to keep a steady balance.

As you're learning about this process, it can be helpful to create a list of the things that are life-giving (reservoir-filling) for you. Here are a few ideas to get you started:

1. Listen to music.
2. Soak in the bathtub.
3. Go for a walk.
4. Sing.
5. Play an instrument.
6. Write in your journal.
7. Read.
8. Bike.
9. Go see a movie.
10. Go bowling.
11. Have a conversation.

12. Call a good friend.
13. Dance.
14. Have a massage.
15. Sit or lie in the sun.
16. Watch funny videos on YouTube.
17. Read a magazine or newspaper.
18. Enjoy hobbies.
19. Spend time with a good friend.
20. Practice karate, judo, or yoga.
21. Exercise with an exercise video.
22. Work on your car or bike.
23. Take care of your plants or garden.
24. Go swimming.
25. Play golf.

When we're involved in enjoyable, fun activities, our brains release chemicals that replenish and rejuvenate us—dopamine, endorphins, and serotonin. This infusion improves our health emotionally, physically, and spiritually. The abundant life Jesus talked about (John 10:10) is an overflowing life, and we can't overflow if we've allowed our resources to run dry. So keep your reservoir well-supplied.

Getting into a Rut of Anxiety or Depression

Depression will rob your joy consistently, and for many, an anxious or depressed state has become so normal that they don't even realize it. For example, I was deeply affected by a chronic illness for many years, to the extent that I was significantly debilitated. During that time, I overheard two people talking about me. One woman said, "Wow, she's really depressed. Do you think she needs to be on an antidepressant?" This was a total surprise to me. I'd gotten used to my melancholy state and didn't even see it for what it was. This comment prompted me to consult with a medical professional and a counselor and to take needed action.

Sometimes we need an outsider to help us troubleshoot and figure out if our anxiety or depression needs to be addressed by a specific game-plan. If you think this might be true for you, talk to a trusted friend, family member, pastor, counselor, or medical professional. Along with these individuals, there are special groups and books that might be very helpful for you. Don't rob yourself of joy by failing to take action.

Comparison

This is a crafty robber of joy that many of us experience. We lose sight of this simple perspective: we have our strengths and weaknesses, and others have their strengths and weaknesses. We have our seasons to shine or to struggle, and others have their seasons to shine or struggle. We get into trouble when we compare others' strengths with our weaknesses and others' strong seasons with our bland or difficult ones.

When I'm struggling with this, God brings to mind the example of Jesus when He talked to Peter, as recorded in John 21:18–22 (NASB):

> "Truly, truly, I say to you, when you were younger, you used to gird yourself and walk wherever you wished; but when you grow old, you will stretch out your hands and someone else will gird you, and bring you where you do not wish to go." Now this He said, signifying by what kind of death he would glorify God. And when He had spoken this, He said to him, "Follow Me!" Peter, turning around, saw the disciple whom Jesus loved following them; the one who also had leaned back on His bosom at the supper and said, "Lord, who is the one who betrays You?" So Peter seeing him said to Jesus, "Lord, and what about this man?" Jesus said to him, "If I want him to remain until I come, what is that to you? You follow Me!"

Peter was falling into our common trap when he looked around and compared himself to someone else—to John, in this case. Jesus' simple answer is His answer to each of us when we fall into this trap: "You follow me!" We need to put on horse-blinders that block our view from comparing ourselves to others and look to Jesus for His unique design, plans, and purposes for us. When we compare ourselves to anyone else, we've found a definite way to diminish our joy.

Perfectionism

Perfectionism is the tendency to be displeased with anything that's not perfect or doesn't meet very high standards.

The problem with being a perfectionist is that you drive yourself and those around you crazy by trying to meet unrealistic goals. This includes things like trying to keep your house super-clean or being unhappy with your spouse or children because they don't measure up to your very high (unrealistic) standards. Perfectionism ultimately robs you of contentment and joy.

Perfectionism often stems from trying to control anxiety. Experience has taught the perfectionist that it feels good and calming to put things in their place or to do things really well. Without realizing it, the perfectionist can be utilizing this method to control underlying tension.

One practical strategy that can help a perfectionist is to set a goal of doing most things *good enough.* In this way, the perfectionist comes to realize that their *good enough* efforts usually result in doing something well, but without the burden of feeling driven. For example, when a recovering perfectionist cleans her house because company's coming, her default setting is to do it perfectly, wearing herself out, and sacrificing other priorities in the process. Instead, she might say to herself, *I'm going to clean each room good enough.* So when she looks at the living room, she might notice that the surfaces don't really need dusting; therefore, she won't automatically clean them. Similarly, she might only spot-vacuum the carpet in areas that really need it. In the bathroom, she might just lightly rinse out the sink with water, rather than giving it a deep cleaning. If you're a perfectionist, it may be causing you anxiety just to think of cleaning in such a quick, imperfect way. Let me encourage you to set out on a journey to be freed from perfectionism. As a result, you'll, give yourself and those around you the gifts of greater happiness and peace.

Questions to Ponder and Discuss

- What are some reasons you allow your schedule to become too intense?
- What helps keep your reservoir full emotionally? Spiritually? Physically?
- How would you know if it was time to seek help for anxiety or depression?
- Has perfectionism been a problem for you or someone close to you? Describe how doing things *good enough* could provide a sense of freedom.

Notes

Week Four

Prepare Your Heart and Mind

Prepare yourself for this week's adventures by reading the following passage. Before you begin, pray that God will speak to you as you think about these verses. Underline words and phrases that express to you joy, positivity, and well-being. Read the passage again, and write down any changes you'd like to see in your life based upon these verses. Read it one more time, jotting down any other observations, comments, questions, or applications that come to mind. Use this book or your journal to record your thoughts.

> Shout for joy to the Lord, all the earth.
> Worship the Lord with gladness;
> come before him with joyful songs.
> Know that the Lord is God.
> It is he who made us, and we are his;
> we are his people, the sheep of his pasture.
> Enter his gates with thanksgiving
> and his courts with praise;
> give thanks to him and praise his name.
> For the Lord is good and his love endures forever;
> his faithfulness continues through all generations
> (Ps. 100 NIV).

Notes

Day 16: Think Thankfully Through Your Day

> In everything give thanks; for this is God's will for you in Christ Jesus (1 Thess. 5:18 NASB).

> You're halfway through your month of creating a new habit of joy; good job! Something that might help or enhance your journey is to read the next day's activity the night before. You might find it helpful to leave the book open in a place where you see it when you first wake up in order to get your day off to a happier start.

Stop what you're doing and look around. Right where you are, stop and find three items that represent some things you're grateful for. In most settings, you can find at least three things: representations of family, health, material items, or schedule. As I write this, I see things that make me thank God for my good health, my Marine son who recently returned home safely from an overseas deployment, and beautiful weather after weeks of gloom. And yet, our minds typically overlook the obvious sources of joy and appreciation. So, throughout this day, pause regularly to notice what you're thankful for. Think of categories like:

- your family
- personal life
- work
- school
- friends
- your country
- surroundings
- past blessings

Then, express appreciation to people and definitely to God. Your cup of joy will overflow as *you* overflow with appreciation. Don't forget to record your list of items throughout the day, and then savor them at night.

Notes

Day 17: Treasure Your Favorites

I thank my God every time I remember you (Phil. 1:3 NIV).

Who has made you feel loved and appreciated? Throughout this day, think of several people who've made you feel valued, loved, or affirmed. Take time with each, thinking through happy scenarios and memories and the affirmation communicated to you. Then, formulate a positive phrase about yourself that their words, deeds, or actions communicated about you. Some examples might be:

1. Dad: I loved fishing with him, the way he cheered me on in all my activities, and his friendly companionship. He always said, "You're my special girl." His overall message to me was, *You are loveable and highly valuable.*
2. My friend, Doug: I've enjoyed sports and video games with him. He's like the brother I never had. His overall message has been, *You'll accomplish great things in life.*
3. My sister: I loved playing games with her, hanging out with neighborhood friends together, and the music we have enjoyed. Our time together has communicated that I am fun, lovable, and safe with her. Her overall message in my life has been, *We're in life together, never alone.*
4. My co-worker, Chris: She's always happy to see me at work, and her words and attitudes convey that I'm doing a good job. She makes me feel like I'm capable, reliable, and skilled. Her message is, *You do a great job!*

Thank and praise God for what each person has contributed to your life. This can be like partaking of little treats all through the day.

Notes

Day 18: Compliment Craze

> Like apples of gold in settings of silver is a word spoken in right circumstances (Prov. 25:11 NASB).

All around us, spiritual beings are moving about in our midst each day, possessing great strengths and resources; they're called people. And you possess something that can fuel them to new heights: positive verbal feedback. You can give verbal gifts today that will strengthen, revitalize, and bring joy.

Throughout your day, look for positive things in others to tell them about. In some cases, a brief sentence will be just right. At other times, a few sentences or even a paragraph will be called for. As I think ahead through my coming day and the people who'll probably cross my path, I'm envisioning a cheerful face, a trendy dresser, a hard-working student, an outstanding employee, and someone with a great sense of humor. I can hardly wait to tell them so!

How about you? Who can you bless, strengthen, fortify, and encourage today? Go and spread your bliss, and don't be surprised when you experience bliss in return.

Notes

Day 19: Music!

> Sing and make music in your heart to the Lord (Eph. 5:19 NIV).

Snow White was right. "Whistle while you work!"

Fill your day with your favorite music. Listen to your kind of music on any device. If you have time, make a playlist of songs or artists. Print out a few sheets with lyrics to songs you like, and sing in your house or car. Memorize words to a song throughout your day.

Do you play an instrument? Make a special effort to play it for a while today. How about dancing? Partake in a little movement in whatever way you're comfortable, whether it's dancing through your house, grabbing a partner for a song or two in the evening, or doing some jazz aerobics. Be proactive to incorporate music into your day. Humming and whistling are allowed, too. Partake plentifully in whatever draws you to enjoy God's happy gift of music.

Notes

Day 20: Best Memories of the Year

> You will be blessed in the city and blessed in the country ...You will be blessed when you come in and blessed when you go out (Deut. 28:3, 6 NIV).

> Just as a problem shared is a problem halved, so happiness shared is happiness doubled. Tell someone about your day's joyful adventure, whether in person, on the phone, or via social media.

This past year, you've experienced highs and lows. Focus on the highs today—the portion of your glass that's full. They don't have to be astronomical highs; they can be warm glows or pleasant memories.

You don't have to stick to just the last twelve months; think generally in terms of the last one-to-two years.

One way to do this is to think in categories. For example, think of the important people in your life: parents, children, spouse, significant others, friends. What has been good regarding them over the last year or so? What about your job, health, trips, holidays, church, nation, and personal growth? Think both in broad strokes and in smaller details about general highs in each of these areas. Write these down as you go so you can savor them at the end of the day, as well as imbed the habit more thoroughly into your being. Here are a few examples:

- My Dad and I had so much fun going to baseball games this past year.
- I've loved my lunches with good friends: Taylor, Shawn, and Chris.
- It was great getting a new car after my old one was a problem for so long.
- Seeing my child excel in Math was wonderful.

- My trip to the mountains was so enjoyable.
- Reading a novel I loved was rewarding.
- I'm enjoying starting to work in this department.

Don't forget that your goal is to spread these thoughts throughout your day, to transform your thought patterns, and to pull these patterns up to the positive as they try to sag through the hours. If you find yourself forgetting, designate a few times to keep you on target: waking, meals, driving, bedtime, etc.

Now enjoy your day as you savor your year.

Notes

My Lifelong Journey →

Did that thought | Still my joy

① • Trust in You, LORD
Outcome comes from You
Help me: Believe This LORD

Teach me to recognize the little foxes that are ruining my vineyard - my ♡ - my attitude

② • STAY IN The Present
• Don't relive what someone has said or done
• Don't worry about what I said or did

Mindfulness Exercises
Day 2/12/15/27

③ I was designed to live outdoors ∴
Regularly GO OUTSIDE WALK THE DOGS!!!

④ Beware of a my Critical Spirit
a Judgemental Spirit
VS Life Love Giving Lens

Help me STOP Thinking:
⊙ everyone shld think + act like me
• Realize people have other viewpoints/agendas/are in diff seasons of their life
• Realize people come from diff backgrds

⑤ Let me live every moment in YOUR Presence
You are my day to day/moment to moment companion

What's coming - Planning - Worries

- I am tired of the constant action items that don't seem to be accomplished
- I am sad the boys have left home
- I am glad the boys have left home
- I am overwhelmed by my Mother + Dad's stuff
- I am scared I won't have enough guests @ the Banquet
- I am fried juggling all the details of my job
-

2.18.19

ENJOY MY EXISTENCE
MOMENT BY MOMENT

Week 5

A Lifestyle of Joy: Principal 5—
Joy – Robbers, Part Two

Remember that thief who comes to "steal and kill and destroy"? (John 10:10) One of the most effective ways to avoid being robbed is to be alert to the possibility and have safeguards in place. Here are a few more joy-robbers to be aware of and to guard against.

People-Pleasing

People-pleasers yearn for validation from others. Their feelings of security and self-confidence are based upon getting approval from others. Therefore, the pleaser's inner security and well-being are dangerously at risk, always depending upon how validated the pleaser feels from people.

As a child, the pleaser may have had a parent who was critical, difficult, or even frightening. Therefore, the only way the child could feel secure was to be sure that the parent was pleased, and this continues to be the default setting for the pleaser as an adult in small and large ways. The journey to freedom from this condition involves personal growth through things like reading specific material about it, healthy relationships, and counseling.

People-pleasing involves a fear of people—the fear that *they won't like me* or *they will hurt me*. A helpful perspective for pleasers is found in Proverbs 29:25–26:

> The fear of man brings a snare, but he who trusts in the Lord will be exalted. Many seek the ruler's favor, but justice for man comes from the LORD (NASB).

This verse helps people to realize that it's only God who can consistently provide us with validation, security, love, safety, and favorable decisions. These are the things pleasers are subconsciously seeking. Through personal growth and time, people-pleasers can learn a lifestyle of resting in these truths about God.

Failing to Live *In the Moment*

Very often, we're living in the past or in the future. Instead of experiencing the exact moment we're living in, we're thinking about what's coming this afternoon or tonight, planning for the weekend, or worrying about something we said yesterday or what was said to us. In this way we're not experiencing the wonder, contentment, or enjoyment that our current moment might bring us. Mindfulness exercises can be very helpful in retraining your brain to live in the present moment. Mindfulness can be described as the gentle effort to be continuously present with whatever you're currently experiencing. Many books are filled with exercises to learn this habit, and some of the mini-adventures in this book are examples of mindfulness exercises (Days 2, 12, 15, and 27). The more you proactively practice mindfulness, the more it automatically becomes a way of life to savor and enjoy your existence moment-by-moment.

Lack of Being Outdoors

A garden was the ideal environment originally created for humans. We were designed to live outdoors in quite a different reality from our current day-to-day experience. Most people don't stop to think about how their lack of being outdoors may be affecting their overall level of joy.

So try an experiment. This week, at different points in your day, try going outside for a few minutes to notice and savor all the outdoor elements: sights, sounds, smells, and both tactile and emotional feelings. (By the way, in doing this, you'll be practicing a mindfulness exercise.) Make a special effort each time you go outdoors to notice if your sense of well-being improves. If it's cold outside, you can do this experiment by going to your window and looking out or think about it while driving.

Last week as I was writing this book, I was feeling a bit tired and stuck. I decided to step into my backyard for a moment. From the time I entered the outdoor world, I felt new life seeping into me. I looked up at the trees with wind gently moving their leaves. Breathing in fresh air felt invigorating. On my back fence a fat golden cat sat, carefully watching a squirrel a few feet away. The squirrel would twitch its tail teasingly and when the cat would make a slight move forward, the squirrel would dash a few feet up a branch. Then, as the cat settled back down, the squirrel would move back to its original position on the fence. They played this cat-and-squirrel game for the several minutes that I was outside. This humorous natural scene felt life-giving, and I was also invigorated just by being outdoors. Within five minutes, I was back at my computer, typing away with new vigor. I feel revitalized in this way each time I step outside for a few minutes. This effect is multiplied and strengthened even more as a way of life through being outdoors for longer periods.

Scientists inform us of the positive biological effects of being outdoors. Our vitamin D levels go up, the sunlight and fresh air interact with our biochemistry to lift our spirits, our concentration levels improve, and our physical bodies even heal faster. If you don't have time to read scientific journals to prove this for yourself, the simple experiment I described earlier should make you a believer in taking regular time each day to enjoy outdoor replenishment.

Judgmentalism

Judgmentalism can be described as being overly critical in an unhelpful, non-sympathetic way. Judgmental people come across as if everyone should think and act the way they themselves do, and they're unaccepting of people who come from different viewpoints or backgrounds. The result is a negativity that saps energy out of the judgmental person, as well as the one they are judging. The judgmental person probably doesn't realize the negative way this behavior is robbing him/her of joy and energy.

There's a difference between making judgments and judgmentalism. When a teacher talks to a student in a belittling, sarcastic way, most people will make the judgment that this is wrong. When someone robs a bank, most people will make the judgment that this is wrong. In contrast, judgmentalism is an attitude in which a person thinks of others in a condemning, self-righteous way. Before you quickly dismiss yourself from this category, take a moment to ask yourself this question: When you disagree with someone's stance or viewpoint, do you still think of them in a sympathetic, loving, supportive way? If not, then you're depriving yourself of seeing through the life-giving lens of love. Loving others who disagree with us is a gift we give to ourselves, as well as to another.

God-Deprivation

> In Your presence is fullness of joy;
> In Your right hand there are pleasures forever (Ps. 16:11 NASB).

Does this describe your day-by-day experience with God? Do you experience God as your enjoyable moment-by-moment companion? Are His spiritual pleasures a consistent part of your life? It takes a journey to learn to experience God like this, but one that you definitely want to take in order to know abundant joy. One of the most effective ways of learning to do this is through asking God to speak to you each day as you read through books of the Bible. An outstanding mentor in this journey is Sarah Young through her small book (also an app) entitled *Jesus Calling* (Thomas Nelson, 2004). As you read Sarah's brief daily writings, you're coached in a lifestyle of enjoying God's moment-by-moment presence with you. This reality of intimate companionship with God is the crucial foundation for a life of deep joy. The final chapter in this book, *A Joyful Relationship with God*, elaborates on this topic.

Joy-robbers are the little foxes that we need to banish from our lives, "the little foxes that are ruining the vineyards, while our vineyards are in blossom" (Song 2:15 NASB). Each of us has our own variety of foxes that we need to recognize and get rid of. In this way, we'll be set free to bloom and thrive.

Questions to Ponder and Discuss

- How has people-pleasing stolen the joy from you or someone you know?
- Describe a positive experience when you lived *in the moment*.
- Think of a time when you really enjoyed being outdoors. Describe the details of what made it so pleasurable.
- Why does being judgmental rob a person of joy?
- Are there times when you've experienced an enjoyable closeness with God? How did you achieve this, and what did you learn from this that you can apply in the days ahead?

Notes

Week Five

Prepare Your Heart and Mind

Prepare yourself for this week's adventures by reading the following passage. Before you begin, pray that God will speak to you as you think about these verses. Underline words and phrases that express to you joy, positivity, and well-being. Read the passage again, and write down any changes you'd like to see in your life based upon these verses. Read it one more time, jotting down any other observations, comments, questions, or applications that come to mind. Use this book or your journal to record your thoughts.

> In the beginning God created the heavens and the earth. Now the earth was formless and empty, darkness was over the surface of the deep, and the Spirit of God was hovering over the waters. And God said, "Let there be light," and there was light. God saw that the light was good, and he separated the light from the darkness. God called the light "day," and the darkness he called "night." And there was evening, and there was morning—the first day. And God said, "Let there be a vault between the waters to separate water from water." So God made the vault and separated the water under the vault from the water above it. And it was so. God called the vault "sky." And there was evening, and there was morning—the second day. And God said, "Let the water under the sky be gathered to one place, and let dry ground appear." And it was so. God called the dry ground "land," and the gathered waters he called "seas." And God saw that it was good. Then God said, "Let the land produce vegetation: seed-bearing plants and trees on the land

that bear fruit with seed in it, according to their various kinds." And it was so. The land produced vegetation: plants bearing seed according to their kinds and trees bearing fruit with seed in it according to their kinds. And God saw that it was good. And there was evening, and there was morning—the third day. And God said, "Let there be lights in the vault of the sky to separate the day from the night, and let them serve as signs to mark sacred times, and days and years, and let them be lights in the vault of the sky to give light on the earth." And it was so. God made two great lights—the greater light to govern the day and the lesser light to govern the night. He also made the stars. God set them in the vault of the sky to give light on the earth, to govern the day and the night, and to separate light from darkness. And God saw that it was good. And there was evening, and there was morning—the fourth day. And God said, "Let the water teem with living creatures, and let birds fly above the earth across the vault of the sky." So God created the great creatures of the sea and every living thing with which the water teems and that moves about in it, according to their kinds, and every winged bird according to its kind. And God saw that it was good. God blessed them and said, "Be fruitful and increase in number and fill the water in the seas, and let the birds increase on the earth." And there was evening, and there was morning—the fifth day. And God said, "Let the land produce living creatures according to their kinds: the livestock, the creatures that move along the ground, and the wild animals, each according to its kind." And it was so. God made the wild animals according to their kinds, the livestock according to their kinds, and all the creatures that move along the ground according to their kinds. And God saw that it was good. Then God said, "Let us make mankind in our image, in our likeness, so that they may rule over the fish in the sea and the birds in the sky, over the livestock and all the wild animals, and over all the creatures that move along the ground." So God created mankind in his own image, in the image of God he created them; male and female he created them. God blessed them and said to them, "Be fruitful and increase in number; fill the earth and subdue it. Rule over the fish in the sea and the birds in the sky and over every living creature that moves on the ground." Then God said, "I give you every seed-bearing plant on the face of the whole earth and every tree that has fruit with seed in it. They will be yours for food. And to all the beasts of the earth and all the birds in the sky and all the creatures that move along the ground—everything that has the breath of life in it—I give every green plant for food." And it was so. God saw all that he had made, and it was very good. And there was evening, and there was morning—the sixth day (Gen. 1 NIV).

Notes

Day 21: From Half-Empty to Half-Full

> Rejoice always, pray without ceasing, in everything give thanks (1 Thess. 5:16–18 NASB).

Remember that quotation by Oscar Wilde? "Two men looked out through prison bars; one saw mud; the other stars."

Which do you see as you go through the events of your day, mud or stars? Often, our thoughts have been trained to see through a negative lens. Today, retrain your brain to see the stars! When you catch yourself thinking about something from a negative viewpoint, stop and think about what is positive in that situation or person. Here are some ideas to get you started.

- You wake up and it's a rainy day. You hate rain. Instead of dwelling on that, think of the plants outside soaking up refreshment, the ground storing replenishment for the future. Think of the air being washed clean. Then you might enjoy a lighted candle throughout the day and think of how it adds a special ambiance, particularly when the day is darker.
- Your teenage son makes a critical comment. You immediately remind yourself of his good qualities and that overall, he's a good kid.
- Your workplace feels like drudgery. You remind yourself of a time in your own life or someone else's when it was hard to find a job, and you thank God for the money this work provides. Then you intentionally think of two good things you like about the job.

With practice, you can slowly but surely develop the habit of rejoicing in the portion of your glass that's full. Drink deeply!

Notes

Day 22: Laugh at Yourself

A cheerful heart is good medicine (Prov. 17:22 NASB).

Picture yourself in a sitcom throughout this day. Your goal is to view yourself with humor and to lighten up. Pretend you're in a sitcom or humorous movie, and mentally write the scene. For example, if someone criticizes you, think of a light-hearted version of what happened with a witty comeback (but not bitter or sarcastic; this will ultimately pull you down). If you find yourself frustrated in traffic, think of how your situation could be humorously written into a movie. If the day is rainy, picture yourself splashing through puddles, joyously becoming wet. Or you can call a friend and retell an experience, highlighting the humorous perspective of it.

If re-framing events in this way is hard for you, enlist the help of a family member or friend. This is a skill to develop that will enable you to view yourself and life with a lighter heart.

Life is short; you can be a great source of amusement for yourself by looking through a humor-tinted lens.

Notes

Day 23: Create Your Own Oasis

Rest in the Lord (Ps. 37:7 NASB).

Escape to an oasis today. Immerse yourself in tranquility several times as you go along your way. We rob ourselves of joy by the anxiety and stress we experience. Angst can be bubbling beneath the surface in our souls, sapping our energy and we don't even realize it. Today, you'll take mini-vacations to help you let go of stress and enter into greater joy and serenity. Try each of the following approaches at least once today, and then don't forget to use them often in the future. These methods have become such a part of me that I incorporate them throughout my day without even intentionally thinking about it.

1. When you relax your body, it's hard for your thoughts to remain tense. Our bodies relax when we focus on breathing in and out peacefully. Breathe in deeply, slowly, counting to eight. Then, breathe out slowly, thinking, *All the tension in my body is flowing out of me, from the top of my head, all the way down, throughout my body, and out the tips of my toes, and I am becoming more relaxed.* Repeat this a few times.

2. Get your entire body to relax in this next simple exercise that can be done in thirty seconds or ten minutes, depending on how long you have. Think through five of your major muscle groups, relaxing them: your forehead, jaw, shoulders, chest, and buttocks. Close your eyes, and starting with your forehead, identify any tension that's there, and envision it melting like butter in a hot pan. Move down through each of the other areas (jaw, shoulders, chest, and buttocks), relaxing and releasing tension. When you get to your buttocks, imagine the tension flowing away from there down your legs and out of your feet and toes. Now, simply enjoy your state of relaxation.

3. If anxious thoughts crowd into your mind today trying to pull you into stressfulness, try this: think of God standing in front of you with

His arms outstretched. Imagine all the things you're worried about as a bundle in your arms. God is saying, "Will you allow me to carry those for you?" Then imagine yourself transferring your burden completely into God's arms. As you now rest your empty hands in your lap, take a deep breath, let it out slowly, and enjoy the restfulness of allowing God to carry your burdens. "Give all your worries and cares to God, for he cares about you" (1 Peter 5:7 NLT).

Notes

Day 24: Design Your Own Adventure

God … richly supplies us with all things to enjoy (1 Tim. 6:17 NASB).

What would make this day extra enjoyable for you? Think of three things that can smoothly fit into your schedule that bring a smile to your face. If your day is busy, it might be little things like listening to your favorite songs driving to and from work or keeping a lighted, scented candle close to you in your home or workplace. You might decide to gently tickle your child for a few minutes or play with your pet for a while. If you have more flexibility in your schedule, you could call a friend you haven't spoken with lately, ride your bike, play a game you enjoy, or take a walk in a scenic area.

So stop right now to design your day ahead, writing three fun things that bring you pleasure. Here are some ideas.

- Read a favorite book or magazine.
- Watch a movie.
- Go bowling.
- Gently brush your child's hair, then have her brush yours.
- Do a favorite athletic activity.
- Take a warm bubble bath.
- Do an art, craft, or needlework activity.
- At your child's bedtime, tell each other one of your favorite memories.
- Have a meal with someone special.
- Browse in a favorite shopping area or bookstore.
- Go for a drive in a scenic area.
- Dance to a song, alone or with your spouse, children, or friends.

Notes

Day 25: Esteeming Others

> These things I have spoken to you so that My joy may be in you, and that your joy may be made full. This is My commandment, that you love one another, just as I have loved you (John 15:11– 12 NASB).

> Comparing will steal your joy, as will competing. God has given each person unique qualities and strengths. If you find yourself comparing or competing with someone, try reminding yourself of the truths in today's activity. Also try thinking of one of that person's strengths, then think of one of your strengths. Then do this again. Rest in the fact that God has gifted each one of us, and that we are each equally loved and valued by Him to the greatest extent possible, because He paid the highest price for us through His Son. And nothing's worth more.

Filling your mind with positive reality is an important part of living a life of joy. But when we feel depressed or anxious, our thoughts can be automatically pulled to notice and dwell upon the negative, especially regarding people. In a vicious cycle, this makes us more depressed, negative, and anxious.

So how about reversing that process today? How about filling your mind with positive truths about people in your life? Some things are true of all people, and these truths are an important framework to establish and revisit in your mind. Review the list below several times today, focusing upon specific people you encounter or know, even those you don't like. Copy this list or carry this book, and review the items, placing someone's name in each blank. By doing this, you'll be thinking about people as God does, and experiencing His joy along the way.

1. God created ________________ in His image; he or she is His masterpiece.
2. ________________ is deeply loved by God.
3. God paid the highest price for ________________. He gave His Son so that ________________ can live with Him forever. The fact that the highest price was paid for ________________ reflects the great worth that God has given him.
4. God made ________________ completely unique. Just as there are no two snowflakes exactly alike, there's no other person like ________________. I can enjoy the fact that this person is a one-of-a-kind portrait. I can enjoy ________________'s uniqueness.
5. ________________ has unique gifts and strengths. I can enjoy these. Two of his or her strengths are ________________ and ________________.
6. Like everyone, ________________ has weaknesses. This in no way reflects upon or robs this person of worth or value.
7. I enjoy the achievements and progress that ________________ makes, without concluding that he or she is more valuable than I am as a person.
8. I like ________________, without comparing this person to myself.
9. I can forgive ________________ for his or her mistakes.
10. ________________ is deeply cherished and treasured by the King ofthe universe.

Notes

Week 6

A Lifestyle of Joy: Principle 6—Playfulness

You've been playing your way through five weeks of adventures now. Have you considered making playfulness a consistent part of your life from this point on? There was a time when I would have been doubtful about this idea. I thought it was shallow and far down on my priority list to be proactive about including fun and playfulness in my schedule. I was proud to be goal-oriented and focused, dedicating myself only to lofty causes and priorities, and I was inwardly critical of people who focused too much on fun and enjoyment. Then I got very sick and was debilitated for several years.

Through this time, as I desperately pieced together a successful plan for restoring my health, I came to learn how important fun and play are to our physical, emotional, and spiritual strength. For our bodies and minds to stay healthy and to flourish, we need to thrive on the biochemicals released when we're involved in pleasure. At work, we're even more productive when our bodies have been fueled and nourished by these biochemicals that were released in our bodies during times of fun.

When I look at the world's creation, it seems that God modeled the quality of playfulness when He created things like toucans, kangaroos, and monkeys. He created us in His image, and playfulness is part of this. No two creatures are ever exactly alike, and human beings can have vastly different preferences along the smorgasbord of options for having fun. One person loves snowboarding, while another loves playing the violin. Photography is enjoyable for some, while others delight in dancing. For some of us, it takes time and experimentation to discover what's fun and restorative. If you find that you need to explore your options for fun and re-creation, all you need is a commitment to this enjoyable discovery process. And of course, you can involve family and friends along the way.

Kids know how to play without ever being taught, but for adults, this ability can slowly fade into nothingness over time. However, once you've started tasting it again in significant doses, your natural ability kicks back in. Then it starts overflowing into the goings-on in your daily life, making you happier and more effective in everything you do.

If you find yourself needing some ideas to get started, here are a few:

1. Choose playful ideas for your exercise options. Get involved in a sport that's truly fun for you. You might add enjoyable outdoor activities to your exercise menu. You could skate or join a hiking group. Dance-type workouts like Zumba or Jazzercise have attracted many people simply because the participants have so much fun.
2. Take a class in something that you find pleasurable: art, photography, music, kayaking, bowling, golf, kite-flying, dancing, crafts, needlework, writing, woodwork, etc.
3. Play games with people: cards, board games, even charades. Utilize *Meet-Up* online or as a phone app to find game-playing groups in your area, or start one and invite your circles.
4. Dance: bebop around your house when no one's looking or when you're out with your spouse or friends. It's a known dopamine booster.
5. If you have a pet, play with him more often in the house, out on walks, or even swimming.
6. Take an improv class. The theme of these classes is playfulness. This is my own personal choice, and I highly recommend it.

Now, if you want to truly become a playfulness aficionado, infusing even more life-giving biochemicals throughout your body, seek to incorporate a playful spirit into the things you do throughout your day. Your mini-adventures have given you a taste of what this can be like.

Someone once said, "Too much fun is just barely enough!" My husband and I often quote this to one another in the spirit of what I've described in this chapter. We do this because, left to ourselves, we can become too serious, overworked, driven, and grim. When that happens, we become drained, irritable, and unhealthy—and that's no fun for us or anyone around us.

Questions to Ponder and Discuss

1. Which end of the spectrum do you naturally go toward, being a person who focuses on work and goals, or a person who naturally seeks fun and play? What have been the benefits and costs of your natural tendency in this regard?
2. What types of play and fun did you enjoy as a child and teenager? Are these things you still find enjoyable as an adult? If you've discontinued them, are there ways you can seek to incorporate some of these now into your adult life?
3. Describe your reaction when you read the phrase, "Too much fun is just barely enough!" Do you embrace this philosophy, or do you have concerns that it might somehow be negative? Describe what a balanced life of work and play would be like for you.
4. What are two things you can do this week to incorporate fun and play into your life?

Notes

Week Six

Prepare Your Heart and Mind

Prepare yourself for this week's adventures by reading the following passage. Before you begin, pray that God will speak to you as you think about these verses. Underline words and phrases that express to you joy, positivity, and well-being. Read the passage again, and write down any changes you'd like to see in your life based upon these verses. Read it one more time, jotting down any other observations, comments, questions, or applications that come to mind. Use this book or your journal to record your thoughts.

> Praise the Lord, my soul. Lord my God, you are very great; you are clothed with splendor and majesty. The Lord wraps himself in light as with a garment; he stretches out the heavens like a tent and lays the beams of his upper chambers on their waters. He makes the clouds his chariot and rides on the wings of the wind. He makes winds his messengers, flames of fire his servants. He set the earth on its foundations; it can never be moved. You covered it with the watery depths as with a garment; the waters stood above the mountains. But at your rebuke the waters fled, at the sound of your thunder they took to flight; they flowed over the mountains, they went down into the valleys, to the place you assigned for them. You set a boundary they cannot cross; never again will they cover the earth. He makes springs pour water into the ravines; it flows between the mountains. They give water to all the beasts of the field; the wild donkeys quench their thirst. The birds of the sky nest by the waters; they sing among the branches. He waters the

mountains from his upper chambers; the land is satisfied by the fruit of his work. He makes grass grow for the cattle, and plants for people to cultivate—bringing forth food from the earth: wine that gladdens human hearts, oil to make their faces shine, and bread that sustains their hearts. The trees of the Lord are well watered, the cedars of Lebanon that he planted. There the birds make their nests; the stork has its home in the junipers. The high mountains belong to the wild goats; the crags are a refuge for the hyrax. He made the moon to mark the seasons, and the sun knows when to go down. You bring darkness, it becomes night, and all the beasts of the forest prowl. The lions roar for their prey and seek their food from God. The sun rises, and they steal away; they return and lie down in their dens. Then people go out to their work, to their labor until evening. How many are your works, Lord! In wisdom you made them all; the earth is full of your creatures. There is the sea, vast and spacious, teeming with creatures beyond number—living things both large and small. There the ships go to and fro, and Leviathan, which you formed to frolic there. All creatures look to you to give them their food at the proper time. When you give it to them, they gather it up; when you open your hand, they are satisfied with good things. When you hide your face, they are terrified; when you take away their breath, they die and return to the dust. When you send your Spirit, they are created, and you renew the face of the ground. May the glory of the Lord endure forever; may the Lord rejoice in his works—he who looks at the earth, and it trembles, who touches the mountains, and they smoke. I will sing to the Lord all my life; I will sing praise to my God as long as I live. May my meditation be pleasing to him, as I rejoice in the Lord. But may sinners vanish from the earth and the wicked be no more. Praise the Lord, my soul. Praise the Lord (Ps. 104 NIV).

Notes

Day 26: I Love My Life Because …

> … the goodness of the Lord in the land of the living (Ps. 27:13 NASB).

Her words slapped me in the face: "I love my life because …" I hardly heard the rest of her sentence because those first five words struck me with such force. She loves her life. Lately, I had been stuck in a pattern of thinking about what was negative in my life. But as I reflected on it a little more and refocused my lens, I realized that I did have a lot to love in my life. I love my life because I was born and raised in a country of abundance and opportunity. I love my life because I was raised by parents who loved and provided for me. I love my life because I experience it as the daughter of the King of the universe. I love my life because I have three wonderful children.

What about you? Throughout your day, pause and complete this sentence, "I love my life because …" Do this at least five times, and with each thing you think of, pause and reflect on what that means for you. Soak in memories, visualize examples, bask in these things that are true, honorable, right, pure, lovely (Phil. 4:8). Thank God for each one.

Notes

Day 27: Enjoy Every Morsel

> So I commend the enjoyment of life, because nothing is better for a man under the sun than to eat and drink and be glad. Then joy will accompany him in his work all the days of the life God has given him under the sun (Eccl. 8:15 NIV).

Today's adventure is the tastiest of them all! Today you'll especially enjoy what you eat. How? Through the skills you've been learning this past month—noticing and savoring. Each time you eat today, intentionally experience your food through each of your five senses. With that first cup of tea or coffee, look at the cup and enjoy its color and shape. Savor the ebony or caramel-colored liquid. Listen to the familiar and inviting sound as you pour it into the cup. Breathe in its tantalizing aroma through your sense of smell. Enjoy the tactile feeling of warmth and comfort as you notice it on your lips and tongue. Finally, relish its delicious taste, continuing to savor this experience through your five senses until that last sip.

Now, during your day, enjoy your food and drink in this same way through each of your senses. Think about God's creation of the varying aspects of your food. Envision coffee beans growing on a bushy plant, stalks of wheat gently swaying in the wind that became the bread in your sandwich, or ripe red apples in an orchard that made their way into your fruit salad. Ponder God's creativity and love in providing these wonderful gifts for you to enjoy.

You'll probably need to place stick-up notes where you eat to remind yourself of today's focus because we aren't in the habit of thinking in this way; it's easy to forget. And don't be hard on yourself. If you realize halfway through your meal that you've forgotten, gently direct your thoughts toward savoring. Your goal is to bring a little extra joy to your day, not to pull yourself down through perfectionism or stringency.

So eat, drink, and be merry today! God "richly supplies us with everything for our enjoyment" (1 Tim. 6:17 NIV).

Notes

Day 28: Picture Pleasures

> He makes springs pour water into the ravines, it flows between the mountains. They give water for all the beasts of the field; the wild donkeys quench their thirst. The birds of the sky nest by the waters; they sing among the branches … How many are your works, LORD! In wisdom you made them all. The earth is full of your creatures (Ps. 104:10–12, 24 NIV).

In each day there are moments that, if frozen in time, can fill you with joy and meaning. Capture those moments in a mental picture.

You're driving to work and see a patch of yellow flowers by the roadside. Take a mental snapshot of the scene and savor its beauty. You're in a store and see a mother bending over, patiently reasoning with her daughter about a toy. Capture the image in your mind and enjoy that Norman Rockwell moment. As I write this, I'm gazing out my window at a winter branch with a few leaves and berries swaying in the wind. My mental camera stores it for my mind's photo album.

Enjoy this secret inner playground today. If it's easy for you, actually take some pictures with your smart phone or digital camera. Be sure to treasure them for a few moments after taking each one, and look back at them at the end of the day for a little mental feast. But mostly, just enjoy the adventure of your day with pictorial gifts you give yourself along the way.

Notes

Day 29: God and . . .

Jesus answered, "It is written …" (Matt. 4:4 NIV).

Last month I felt very lonely. My husband and I had just moved to a new state, and he needed to go on a trip overseas for three weeks. I felt fine about this when we planned it several months in advance; I'm usually independent and self-sufficient. But in this new city, I didn't yet know many people, and after about ten days in my quiet house, loneliness began to overwhelm me. At first I tried keeping the radio on, watching TV, and making some long-distance phone calls. It took me a while to remember a skill I'd learned decades before: treating my negative situation or emotion with the ointment of God's truth about Himself, contrasting my difficulty with the beauty of one of God's specific attributes. When I did this regarding the feeling of loneliness, my world changed.

For example, I remembered, "Do not fear, for I am with you. Do not be dismayed, for I am your God. I will strengthen you and help you; I will uphold you with my righteous right hand" (Isa. 41:10 NASB). I thought about the fact that God is with me always, closer than my breath, ready with all of His resources to help me. I started talking to Him throughout my day, laughing with Him, singing songs to Him, envisioning sitting next to Him with my head on His shoulder as He gently stroked my hair. I was no longer sad or lonely.

So today, try contrasting negative situations with the positivity of specific verses and God's specific attributes. Then talk to Him and praise Him about this. If you experience an ongoing, troubling relationship with someone, remind yourself that God is close, perfect, and righteous; He is always available, ready to comfort you (Jer. 31:3). If you're struggling financially, remind yourself that God is totally in control, available with His wisdom to help you (James 1:2–5). If the day is dark and gloomy, spend time thinking about the fact that God is light, and there is no darkness in Him (1 John 1:5). If you feel like a failure, remind yourself of God's never-ending mercy, acceptance, patience, and power to help you change (Ps. 18). Finding applicable Bible verses is immensely helpful, and search engines now make it so easy.

Look for ways to savor God's invisible truths, which are more accurate than what we see, feel, and experience in this visible realm.

Notes

Day 30: Notice, Pray, Thank, Praise

It is more blessed to give than to receive (Acts 20:35 NASB).

> Every oak tree started out as a nut that decided to stand its ground. As you're approaching the end of your thirty-one days, rejoice in whatever progress you've made. Even if you're not as far along as you'd like, you're farther than when you started. The last two sections of the book will give you more ideas to grow in this process you've begun. "By perseverance the snail reached the ark." (Charles Spurgeon)

Today, you'll be a secret agent, and your mission will be to dispense blessings on unsuspecting victims. Your goal is to select several individuals whom you encounter throughout your day and pray for them, knowing that you can make astronomical changes in their lives through your words spoken to God on their behalf. Do you doubt the reality of that possibility? Another special agent who knew this topic well has written to us, "You do not have, because you do not ask God" (James 4:2 NIV). So ask great things for the people you come across. Then thank and praise God for each person.

You're at the grocery store? Pray for the cashier to experience God's love and presence in a special way. Thank God for providing her with this job, and praise Him for His lavish love for her.

You're at a meeting with someone who irritates you. Pray that God will guide him in his marriage and family, and ask God to give him wisdom in his work and life decisions. Thank and praise God for the unique gifts He has given this person.

You're watching a television show that features a well-known actor. Pray that this person will come into a close relationship with

God. Thank and praise God that He created and designed this person in His love.

And of course, if family or friends are your unsuspecting recipients, you'll be able to pray and thank God very specifically for things you know about them.

Have fun as you go about your mission today. And of course, you will be paid generously. "Give, and it will be given to you. A good measure, pressed down, shaken together and running over, will be poured into your lap. For with the measure you use, it will be measured to you" (Luke 6:38 NASB). The "good measure" you receive may very well be overflowing joy.

Notes

Day 31: Think Thankfully through Your Life

... overflowing with thankfulness (Col. 2:7 NIV).

It's been proven scientifically that thankfulness makes us healthier. Gratitude improves emotional and physical health. So says a study by Dr. Robert Emmons at the University of California, Davis. Being thankful will make us healthier and happier, not to mention that gratitude helps to facilitate a sweeter relationship with God, which is of primary importance.

Thankfulness is a gift we can give to God or to another that ultimately comes back as a gift to ourselves. God really has designed us well.

But how? How do we make gratitude a strong habit in our daily lives? Through intentional practice. You've come a long way toward developing this pattern over these past weeks.

Today, continue your joyful journey by reflecting on the things you're most thankful for. During different parts of your day, comb through each of your decades one by one, savoring a few things in each of them that you're thankful for. Treasure your thoughts with God, delight in their details, and rejoice with your loving Father. You might also share today's activity with someone over coffee or a meal.

Jot down a phrase to remind you of each item; then look back over your list at the end of the day, bathing your soul in warmth and encouragement. For example:

- Birth to age ten: Moved from Ohio to Florida to Texas. Learned to love change.
- Age ten to twenty: Learned to play piano and attended college.
- Age twenty to thirty: Got married! Loved my job.
- Age thirty to forty: Enjoyed raising three children; enjoyed our move to Oregon.

Dr. Emmons learned in his study that the other-centered act of thankfulness comes back to bless us emotionally and physically. After all, God designed us. His principles are for our good, because He dearly loves us.

Thankfulness—what a simple and beautiful way to live happier and healthier lives and to experience what God intended for us all along. "Rejoice always, pray without ceasing, in everything give thanks, for this is God's will for you in Christ Jesus" (1 Thess. 5:16–18 NASB).

Notes

The Road Ahead

Go Ahead, Indulge!

Well done! You've come a long way toward creating your new, joy-filled life. Now, like a young rosebush that has just produced its first blossoms, your new lifestyle needs ongoing nurturance, feeding, and care in order to thrive. Here are a few ideas to help.

- Repeat your thirty-one-day adventure. A fun trip is worth taking again. Each activity is actually a skill that can become a part of your natural way of thinking, providing your brain with a daily smorgasbord to choose from, without even consciously trying. If you haven't already, enlist friends or family to come with you on this journey.
- After repeating your thirty-one-day adventure, try this for the following month: At the beginning of each day, choose two or three activities to combine for that day. For example, you might choose to do Picture Pleasures and Complement Craze. As before, you could carry a reminding note card around with these categories written on it. Combining several mental activities throughout your day gets easier the more you do it. It can be like giving yourself a mental trip to Disneyland, choosing a different set of rides each time.
- After a while, you'll be ready to pick and choose randomly from all thirty-one activities as you've installed them into your mental computer. You'll find yourself going to different ones by default without even thinking about it, while reaping joyful, adventuresome benefits.

Even More Joy

Just as a rosebush needs foundational elements to grow and thrive, your life needs foundational components to create the health that overflows into a lifestyle of joy. Here's a checklist of some necessary ingredients for experiencing a transformed, abundant life. Put a check by the ones you most need to nurture.

- ○ Begin a personal relationship with God that's growing and deepening.
- ○ Have daily time interacting with God through reading the Bible and praying.
- ○ Establish a supportive group of friends who walk through life with you, sharing your joys and struggles.
- ○ Become part of a healthy, biblical church, where you're involved in both giving and receiving in God's kingdom.
- ○ Get professional counseling for deeper issues that are hindering you.

Stop now and pray for each area you checked above for God's guidance and provision as you seek to grow in strength in each of them. Then choose one that seems the most important to you, and begin to take small steps to strengthen that area. Many small steps will eventually bring you to your destination.

If you checked the first point about beginning a personal relationship with God, the next section will explain how to experience this area of joy.

A Joyful Relationship with God

Many people go through life not experiencing their fullest capacity for joy because of a hindered relationship with God. It's so important to know that God loves you dearly and wants to relate to you intimately in this life and for all of eternity. Jesus Christ came to this planet so that each of us could know and understand God in a personal way. So why is it hard for us to experience this?

When Jesus came to this earth, He explained that each person is separated from God by *sin*. This is actually an ancient Greek archery term meaning to fall short of the mark. Simply put, this means that God originally designed us to live perfect lives in continual communication with Him, but we have each chosen not to do this in small and large ways; we've fallen short of God's mark for us. This has created a separation between us and God, like when we've done something wrong toward someone who loves us but we've never spoken to him/her about it, nor even addressed it. The result of this is spiritual separation from God. Although we may try to get close to God through our own efforts, we inevitably fail because we haven't corrected this foundational wrong. We may try to earn God's acceptance by doing good things in life or through practicing a moral philosophy. But our good efforts are insufficient to solve the problem of our broken relationship with God. So how can we solve this problem?

When Jesus came to the earth, He made the bold statement that no one comes to the Father except through Him (John 14:6). Throughout His life, Jesus explained that people deserve to pay a penalty for their sins. Just as in a court of law the offender pays a price, there's a price for the wrongs we've done. That price is spiritual separation from God, both now and throughout eternity. So that we wouldn't have to live or die separated from God, Jesus Christ died in our place because of His love for us. On the cross, Jesus took all of our sins on Himself and completely paid for them. Peter, one of Jesus's closest disciples, described it in this way, "For Christ also died for sins... the just for the unjust, so that he might bring us to God" (1 Peter 3:18 NASB). Because of Jesus' death on the cross, our sins no longer have to separate us from God.

Jesus not only died for our sins, but He rose from the dead (1 Cor. 15:3–6). When He did this, He proved beyond a doubt that He can rightfully promise eternal life—that He is the Son of God and the only means by which we can know God.

So, instead of trying harder to reach God, Jesus told us how we can begin a relationship with Him. Jesus said, "Come to me. If anyone thirsts, let him come to me and drink. Whoever believes in me... out of his heart will flow rivers of living water" (John 7:37–38 ESV). It was Jesus' love for us that caused Him to endure the cross, and He now invites us to come to Him that we might begin a personal relationship with God.

But just knowing what Jesus has done for us and what He is offering us isn't enough. To have a relationship with God, we need to welcome Him into our lives. We must each individually accept Jesus Christ as our Savior and Lord. Accepting Jesus means believing that Jesus is the

Son of God, whom He claimed to be, then inviting Him to guide and direct our lives. And this is Jesus' invitation to you: "Here I am! I stand at the door and knock. If anyone hears my voice and opens the door, I will come in" (Rev. 3:20 NIV).

So how will you respond to God's invitation? You can begin a personal relationship with God by receiving Christ right now. Here's how: simply ask Him.

The precise words you use to commit yourself to God aren't important. He knows the intentions of your heart. If you're unsure of what to pray, this prayer might help you put it into words:

> *Jesus, I want to know You. I want You to come into my life. Thank You for dying on the cross for my sins so that I could be fully accepted by You. Only You can give me the power to change and become the person You created me to be. Thank You for forgiving me and giving me eternal life with God. I give my life to You. Please make me the kind of person You want me to be. Amen.*

If you sincerely asked Jesus into your life just now, then He has come into your life as He promised. You've begun a personal relationship with God. What follows is a lifelong journey of change, growth, and joy as you get to know Him better through prayer (i.e., talking to Him), Bible study, interaction with other Christians, and living life with God.

To continue exploring this aspect of your joyful journey, there are many helpful things you can do. If you've recently made the decision to begin following God, become involved with a group of fellow-believers so they can walk alongside you. There are numerous beneficial books and websites. One of my favorites is *www.everystudent.com*. Check out its many resources, and enjoy the abundance. Jesus said, "I came that they may have life, and have it abundantly" (John 10:10 NASB). He's all about a joyful, overflowing life. Journey with Him on this eternal expedition of adventure and discovery!

Leading a Discussion Group through *Retrain Your Brain for Joy*

An Eight-Week Study

Retrain Your Brain for Joy is a delightful adventure to experience with a group of people. Like so many journeys, this one can be even more fun and rewarding if you travel and learn with others. Whether your discussion group consists of two, twenty, or two hundred people, the following guidelines will help your group to run more smoothly and joyfully.

An Eight-Week Schedule

I suggest an eight-week format. If your group consists of more than fifteen people, discussion time will be more effective if you divide into two or more smaller groups. Your first meeting together can be a time of getting to know one another and going through the contents of the first section entitled *Come On an Adventure*. Throughout the next six weeks, your study will cover the thirty-one adventures, broken into five adventures per week. The final, eighth week can cover the remaining sections of the book. This final time together can also be an opportunity for people in the study to reflect and review, looking back over their journey and growth throughout this study process.

Week One

The first week that your group meets is a time for everyone to get to know each other and for the leader(s) to introduce the ideas of the book. If the books haven't been distributed before this first meeting, you can do so at this time, or tell members where to get them. The easiest thing for the leaders may be to have the group members order books for themselves by going to either the author's website (*www.maryhenderson.org*) or a bookselling website like Amazon.com.

During this first time together, have the members introduce themselves: their names, profession, family, hobbies they enjoy, etc.

You might then go around the group a second time and have everyone tell about an enjoyable memory from their childhood. Next, go over the content of the opening chapter, *Come on An Adventure*. You can do this, even if the members don't yet have their books. Pause after each section, and ask if anyone has questions or comments.

As leaders, be proactive to establish a warm, lighthearted, and safe atmosphere during this first time together. You might share snacks at the end of the meeting to enable everyone to continue getting to know one another. You want to lay the foundation for enjoyable and positive times of discussion in the weeks ahead.

Weeks Two through Seven

These weeks encompass the bulk of the study in which the group members are actually going through the adventures at home, then coming together to discuss them.

1. I suggest that, as a leader, you start each week by praying aloud for your group's time together.
2. Each week starts with a section explaining a principle for creating a lifestyle of joy: Noticing and Savoring; Can You Say Neuroplasticity?; Out with the Old, in with the New; Joy Robbers—Part One; Joy Robbers—Part Two; and Playfulness. If you want to include a *talk* before your discussion time, you can draw from this section for the content of what you say.

   At the end of each of these sections are some great discussion questions for your group. Don't forget to lead your group in exploring these.

3. Next, each week begins with a portion of Scripture that sets the stage for the week's adventures. Questions are included in the book for your members to think and write about at home:

   Underline words and phrases that express to you joy, positivity, and well-being. Read the passage again, and write down any changes you'd like to see in your life based upon these verses.

Read it one more time, jotting down any other observations, comments, questions, or applications that come to mind.

During your weekly meeting, lead your group in a discussion of these questions. Feel free to add questions you feel might be helpful for the group about the Scripture passage, being mindful of your time management. Lead your group in a rich discussion of God's truths and how they impact the individuals in your group.

4. The remainder of your time each week will be spent going over each adventure. Since each day's adventure starts with a verse, ask the group for their comments or reflections about the passage.

   I suggest that you then read the adventure together, taking turns with different people reading aloud. Then ask the group how this day's adventure went for them, as well as what they experienced and learned. The following are some questions you might use on different days:

   - What was this day's adventure like for you?
   - What did you notice this day?
   - Would anyone like to share what you wrote in your journal for this day's experience?
   - Can you share an example of how you applied this adventure during your week?
   - Was there anything that made it difficult for you to do this day's adventure?
   - Is there anything from your past or growing up experience that made this easier or more difficult for you?

   Some days have sidebars. For example, on Day 1, there's a sidebar about creating a lifelong habit as you lay your head on your pillow each night. As a leader, draw attention to these sidebars, either through your own comments or by asking the group for their thoughts.

5. Close your time each week in prayer. You can pray for the group as a leader, or if you have time, several people can pray for the needs of individuals that may have been expressed in your discussion. Don't forget to thank God for the good things happening in group members' lives and to praise God for various aspects of who He is.

Week Eight

For your final week, go over the sections entitled *Go Ahead, Indulge!, Even More Joy,* and *A Joyful Relationship with God.* Read the first two of these sections aloud as a group, commenting or asking questions along the way. The final section, *A Joyful Relationship with God,* is written for those who haven't (or aren't sure if they've ever) begun a personal relationship with God. During your group time, you can ask if anyone has any questions or comments about this section. Then, if you sense that there are those who are unsure about their personal relationship with God, meet with them individually for a discussion and to answer questions.

You should have some time left after going over these three sections as a group. Ask the members to look back through their books and comment on any of the adventures that particularly stood out for them. In addition, ask how this study has positively impacted their lives and how they can continue to apply what they've learned. As a group, you could end by praying for one another about these things for the days ahead. You might close by sharing a meal or snacks together.

A Word about Time Management

As a leader, you'll want to manage your time carefully each week. Work diligently to keep your group moving along in its discussion so that you can cover everything. This is both an art and a science, with you as a leader giving everyone opportunities to talk. At the same time, create an atmosphere of support and encouragement. Sensitively keep the group moving forward in the interest of time. Also, as a leader you don't want to talk too much yourself. Instead, draw out the discussion from your group members. Pray for yourself and the group as you joyfully juggle all of these balls.

About the Author

Mary Henderson is a Licensed Professional Clinical Counselor and a Licensed Marriage and Family Therapist. She is the author of *Break Free: Journey with God through Chronic Illness to Health.* Mary is the mother of three grown children. She and her husband live in Austin, Texas.

Visit Mary's website: *http://www.maryhenderson.org*, and follow *marykhenderson* on Twitter and *authormaryhenderson* on Facebook.

Adventure Cards

Cut out the following cards and enjoy one per day to correspond with each adventure. You can use the back of the cards to record your thoughts for that day. Punch a hole in the upper left-hand corner, and use a keychain-type ring or a string through the hole to attach the cards together.

Retrain
Your Brain
for Joy
Adventure
Cards

Day 1:
Count Your Many Blessings

Finally, brethren, whatever is true, whatever is honorable, whatever is right, whatever is pure, whatever is lovely, whatever is of good repute, if there is any excellence and if anything worthy of praise, dwell on these things.
Philippians 4:8 (NASB)

Day 2:
Beauty Quest

Every good thing given and every perfect gift is from above, coming down from the Father of lights, with whom there is no variation or shifting shadow.
James 1:17 (NASB)

Day 3:
Notice What You Do Well

I will give thanks to Thee, for I am fearfully and wonderfully made; Wonderful are Thy works, and my soul knows it very well.
Psalm 139:14 (NASB)

Day 4:
Good News!

Like cold water to a weary soul, So is good news from a distant land.
Proverbs 25:25 (NASB)

Day 5: *Best Memories of Your Life* However many years a man may live, let him enjoy them all. Ecclesiastes 11:8 (NASB)	*Day 6:* *Opposite Day* I would have despaired unless I had believed that I would see the goodness of the Lord in the land of the living. Psalm 27:13 (NASB)
Day 7: *Smile!* Bright eyes gladden the heart. Proverbs 15:30 (NASB)	*Day 8:* *Doors Close, New Doors Open* Weeping may last for the night, but a shout of joy comes in the morning. Psalm 30:5 (NASB)

Day 9:
God Sightings

He who has ears to
hear, let him hear.
Matthew 11:15 (NASB)

Day 10:
Give, Give, and Give Again

Each one must do just as he
has purposed in his heart, not
grudgingly or under compulsion,
for God loves a cheerful giver.
2 Corinthians 9:7 (NASB)

Day 11:
Appreciate God Through the ABC's

On the glorious splendor of Your
majesty, And on Your wonderful
works, I will meditate.
Psalm145:5 (NASB)

Day 12:
Delight in Your Day

"But Mary treasured all
these things, pondering
them in her heart."
Luke 2:19 (NASB)

Day 13:
The Strengths of My People

I thank my God in all my remembrance of you.
Philippians 1:3 (NASB)

Day 14:
Statements of Self-Esteem

God created man in His own image, in the image of God He created him; male and female He created them.
Genesis 1:27 (NASB)

Day 15:
Live in the Moment

Therefore do not worry about tomorrow, for tomorrow will worry about itself. Each day has enough trouble of its own.
Matthew 6:34 (NASB)

Day 16:
Think Thankfully Through Your Day

In everything give thanks; for this is God's will for you in Christ Jesus.
1 Thessalonians 5:18 (NASB)

Day 17: ***Treasure Your Favorites*** I thank my God every time I remember you. Philippians 1:3 (NIV)	***Day 18:*** ***Compliment Craze*** A word aptly spoken is like apples of gold in settings of silver. Proverbs 25:11 (NASB)
Day 19: ***Music!*** Sing and make music in your heart to the Lord. Ephesians 5:19 (NASB)	***Day 20:*** ***Best Memories of the Year*** You will be blessed in the city and blessed in the country… You will be blessed when you come in and blessed when you go out Deuteronomy 28:3, 6 (NASB)

Day 21: ***From Half-Empty to Half-Full*** Rejoice always, pray without ceasing, in everything give thanks. 1 Thessalonians 5:16–18 (NASB)	***Day 22:*** ***Laugh at Yourself*** A cheerful heart is good medicine. Proverbs 17:22 (NASB)
Day 23: ***Create Your Own Oasis*** Rest in the Lord. Psalm 37:7 (NASB)	***Day 24:*** ***Design Your Own Adventure*** God… richly supplies us with all things to enjoy. 1 Timothy 6:17 (NASB)

Day 25: Esteeming Others

These things I have spoken
to you so that My joy may
be in you, and that your joy
may be made full. This is My
commandment, that you love one
another, just as I have loved you.
John 15:11,12 (NASB)

Day 26: I Love My Life Because …

… the goodness of the Lord
in the land of the living.
Psalm 27:13 (NASB)

Day 27: Enjoy Every Morsel

So I commend the enjoyment of
life, because nothing is better
for a man under the sun than to
eat and drink and be glad. Then
joy will accompany him in his
work all the days of the life God
has given him under the sun.
Ecclesiastes 8:15 (NASB)

Day 28: Picture Pleasures

He makes springs pour water
into the ravines, it flows
between the mountains. They
give water for all the beasts
of the field; the wild donkeys
quench their thirst. The birds of
the sky nest by the waters; they
sing among the branches …
Psalm 104:10–12 (NASB)

Day 29: *God and . . .* Jesus answered, "It is written ..." Matthew 4:4 (NASB)	*Day 30:* *Notice, Pray, Thank, Praise* It is more blessed to give than to receive. Acts 20:35 (NASB)
Day 31: *Think Thankfully through Your Life* ... overflowing with thankfulness. Colossians 2:7 (NASB)	

CPSIA information can be obtained at www.ICGtesting.com
Printed in the USA
LVOW12s2345211114

414967LV00001B/1/P